Declutter Your Mind

Simple and Effective Strategies to Free Yourself From Anxiety

(Easy Techniques to Incorporate Decluttering in Your Lifestyle for Peace and Happiness)

Chong Rodger

Published By **Andrew Zen**

Chong Rodger

All Rights Reserved

Declutter Your Mind: Simple and Effective Strategies to Free Yourself From Anxiety (Easy Techniques to Incorporate Decluttering in Your Lifestyle for Peace and Happiness)

ISBN 978-1-7774626-9-7

No part of this guidebook shall be reproduced in any form without permission in writing from the publisher except in the case of brief quotations embodied in critical articles or reviews.

Legal & Disclaimer

The information contained in this book is not designed to replace or take the place of any form of medicine or professional medical advice. The information in this book has been provided for educational & entertainment purposes only.

The information contained in this book has been compiled from sources deemed reliable, and it is accurate to the best of the Author's knowledge; however, the Author cannot guarantee its accuracy and validity and cannot be held liable for any errors or omissions. Changes are periodically made to this book. You must consult your doctor or get professional medical advice before using any of the suggested remedies, techniques, or information in this book.

Upon using the information contained in this book, you agree to hold harmless the Author from and against any damages, costs, and expenses, including any legal fees potentially resulting from the application of any of the information provided by this guide. This disclaimer applies to any damages or injury caused by the use and application, whether directly or indirectly, of any advice or information presented, whether for breach of contract, tort, negligence, personal injury, criminal intent, or under any other cause of action.

You agree to accept all risks of using the information presented inside this book. You need to consult a professional medical practitioner in order to ensure you are both able and healthy enough to participate in this program.

Table Of Contents

Chapter 1: Why Your Brain Gets Stuck In Endless Loops 1

Chapter 2: The Benefits Of Mindfulness: How To Train Your Brain To Stop Overthinking" 6

Chapter 3: How Negative Self-Talk Impacts Your Brain And Behavior 10

Chapter 4: How To Stop Overanalyzing And Take Action 14

Chapter 5: Perfectionism: Why Striving For Perfection Can Fuel Overthinking 17

Chapter 6: The Power Of Gratitude 21

Chapter 7: How To Break Free From Repetitive Thoughts 24

Chapter 8: Cognitive Distortions 26

Chapter 9: How To Manage Stress For A Clearer Mind 30

Chapter 10: The Power Of Perspective .. 35

Chapter 11: How To Overcome Analysis Paralysis" 38

Chapter 12: How To Release Negative Thoughts And Embrace Change 42

Chapter 13: How To Improve Your Sleep Habits For A Clearer Mind 45

Chapter 14: The Role Of Exercise In Reducing Over Thinking 49

Chapter 15: How To Eat For A Clearer Mind 53

Chapter 16: The Power Of Creativity 58

Chapter 17: How To Build Relationships That Help Combat Overthinking 61

Chapter 18: The Benefits Of Laughter: How To Use Humor To Combat Overthinking 65

Chapter 19: How To Use Mindfulness Techniques To Reduce Overthinking" 69

Chapter 20: How To Use Positive Self-Talk To Overcome Overthinking" 73

Chapter 21: Understanding Stress 78

Chapter 22: What Is A Stress Trap? 84

Chapter 23: Engaging 85

Chapter 24: What To Do Within The Direction Of Such Instances? 98

Chapter 25: Coping 109

Chapter 26: Rewire Your Memories 125

Chapter 27: Preparing For Cleaning 140

Chapter 28: Basic Cleaning Techniques 148

Chapter 29: Deep Cleaning Tasks 158

Chapter 30: Maintaining A Clean Room 174

Chapter 1: Why Your Brain Gets Stuck In Endless Loops

Do you find out yourself lost in perception, traumatic approximately topics which have already happened or might arise within the destiny? Do you warfare to reveal off your thoughts and loosen up? If so, you may be caught within the overthinking trap.

Overthinking is a commonplace trouble that influences many humans. It takes region while you get stuck in a cycle of repetitive mind, regularly related to worry or tension. The consistent barrage of thoughts may be difficult and overwhelming, main to multiplied strain and tension.

So, why are we able to overthink? The solution lies within the manner our brains are pressured. Our brains are constantly processing facts, taking in stimuli from the sector spherical us and making experience of it. When we stumble upon a trouble or a disturbing state of affairs, our brains kick into excessive gear, searching for an answer or a manner out of the state of affairs.

Unfortunately, this manner can once in a while go awry. When we get stuck in a cycle of overthinking, our brains emerge as hyper-focused on the problem, making it tough to allow pass of the concern and circulate on. This may be in particular authentic for people who are susceptible to tension or who've professional trauma.

Overthinking may additionally moreover have some of bad outcomes at the mind. For one, it could result in increased strain and tension, that can have a bad effect on every our physical and highbrow fitness. Overthinking also can disrupt sleep, fundamental to emotions of exhaustion and fatigue.

Additionally, overthinking can honestly trade the manner our brains function. Studies have verified that folks that have interaction in excessive annoying have increased pastime inside the prefrontal cortex, a part of the brain related to preference-making and trouble-solving. Over time, this prolonged activity can bring about a reduction within the thoughts's ability to hobby and technique data successfully.

So, how are you going to harm free from the overthinking entice? The secret's to discover ways to manipulate your mind and feelings in a healthy manner. Here are some pointers that will help you do absolutely that:

Practice Mindfulness: Mindfulness is the workout of being gift and absolutely engaged in the present day 2d. When you are engaged in mindfulness, you are not concerned about the beyond or destiny, but as an alternative, simply targeted on the present. This can assist reduce overthinking thru manner of allowing you to allow skip of problems and reputation at the prevailing 2nd.

Challenge Your Thoughts: When you locate your self caught in a cycle of overthinking, strive difficult your thoughts. Ask your self in case your issues are sensible and if there may be evidence to assist them. Often, our issues are primarily based on irrational fears and difficult them can assist located topics into mind-set.

Act: If you are caught in a cycle of overthinking, taking motion can assist damage the cycle. Instead of ruminating in your thoughts, take a proactive technique and art work closer to a solution. This can assist lessen your issues and give you a enjoy of control.

Practice Self-Care: Taking care of your self is vital for dealing with overthinking. Make positive you are becoming sufficient sleep, consuming a wholesome weight loss plan, and engaging in normal workout. Additionally, locate time for sports activities you experience and spend time with loved ones.

Exercises to Help Manage Overthinking

Here are some wearing events to help you manage overthinking:

Journaling: Writing down your mind and issues let you advantage attitude and reduce overthinking. Try writing down your problems for 10 minutes each day after which reflecting on them.

Visualization: Visualizing a peaceful scene, which consist of a beach or a mountain top, can assist lessen stress and tension. Take a couple of minutes each day to close your eyes and visualize a non violent scene.

3 Breathing Exercises: Focusing to your breath can help calm your thoughts and decrease overthinking. Try taking deep breaths for a few minutes every day, specializing within the sensation of the air shifting inside and outside of your frame.

Mindful Observation: When you discover your self out of place in concept, attempt working towards aware remark. Focus on the arena round you, taking note of your senses. This can help convey you back to the triumphing moment and reduce overthinking.

Chapter 2: The Benefits Of Mindfulness: How To Train Your Brain To Stop Overthinking"

Overthinking is a common trouble that influences human beings of every age and backgrounds. It can result in a enormous sort of terrible outcomes, which includes tension, pressure, and bodily symptoms and symptoms collectively with headaches and fatigue. However, with the aid of way of training mindfulness, we're capable of teach our brains to break free from the cycle of overthinking and find extra peace and clarity in our lives.

Mindfulness is the workout of bringing our interest to the winning 2d, with reputation and without judgment. It includes paying attention to our mind, feelings, and physical sensations, at the identical time as moreover being aware about the arena spherical us. By training mindfulness, we can learn how to study our thoughts without becoming linked to them, and this could help us smash free from the endless cycle of overthinking.

There are numerous blessings of mindfulness which can assist us triumph over overthinking. Firstly, mindfulness permits us growth more interest of our mind and feelings. We discover ways to take a look at them with out judgment, and which means we're much less likely to grow to be overwhelmed by means of manner of using them. By searching at our thoughts and feelings on this way, we're capable of gain a greater expertise of our very very own thoughts, and this can assist us make bigger more compassion and self-cognizance.

Secondly, mindfulness facilitates us increase extra focus and consciousness. By running in the direction of mindfulness, we teach our brains to be aware of the prevailing 2nd, in choice to turning into distracted by way of way of our thoughts and problems. This manner that we're better able to live centered on one project or concept at a time, and this may assist us be extra efficient and effective in our each day lives.

Thirdly, mindfulness allows us expand greater self-compassion. By training mindfulness, we learn how to address ourselves with kindness and information, in preference to harsh self-judgment. This can assist us triumph over terrible self-speak and increase a extra revel in of self confidence and vanity.

If you're suffering with overthinking, there are various wearing activities you may attempt to include mindfulness into your every day life. One exercising is the body check, in that you lie down or take a seat without problems and produce your attention on your frame. Starting on the side of your ft, test up thru your body, noticing any sensations or regions of tension. Simply observe those sensations with out judgment and observe if you could launch any regions of hysteria as you bypass.

Another exercise is aware respiratory, in which you take a couple of minutes to interest on your breath, noticing the feeling of the air moving interior and out of your body. If your mind wanders, actually deliver your hobby once more for your breath with out judgment.

Finally, you can attempt aware eating, in that you're taking a couple of minutes to devour a snack or meal, paying attention to the flavors, textures, and sensations of the food. Notice any thoughts or emotions that arise, and surely test them without judgment.

The blessings of mindfulness in overcoming overthinking are many. By growing extra focus, consciousness, and self-compassion, we can educate our brains to break unfastened from the cycle of overthinking and discover more peace and readability in our lives. Remember, mindfulness takes workout and staying energy, but the benefits are properly well surely really worth the try.

Chapter 3: How Negative Self-Talk Impacts Your Brain And Behavior

It's smooth to get caught up in horrible self-communicate. We've all completed it earlier than. It's that nagging voice inner our heads that tells us we're now not correct sufficient, smart sufficient, or succesful enough. But did you apprehend that awful self-talk can in reality rewire your mind and reason a pattern of overthinking? In this financial disaster, we can explore the technological statistics inside the lower back of awful self-talk and the way it may impact your brain and conduct. We'll furthermore offer you with techniques to combat it and damage loose from the overthinking entice.

Have you ever observed how horrific self-speak has a tendency to spiral out of control? It starts offevolved offevolved with a easy idea like "I'm no longer actual at this," and earlier than you're privy to it, you're ate up by way of way of using an internet of horrible mind. This happens due to the truth horrible self-talk triggers the discharge of stress hormones like cortisol, that could bring about an boom in tension and rumination. The extra you've got interplay in terrible self-communicate, the more your brain will become burdened out to default to this pattern of overthinking.

But there can be right statistics. Just as bad self-talk can impact your mind and behavior, incredible self-speak can also have a profound impact. Studies have verified that training self-compassion and superb self-communicate can reduce tension, boost shallowness, and enhance normal nicely-being. So, if you find out your self caught in a bad self-talk spiral, attempt moving your mindset to at least one in each of self-compassion and positivity.

One manner to fight bad self-speak is to reframe your thoughts. Instead of focusing on what you're now not right at, awareness on what you are accurate at. Make a list of your strengths and accomplishments and are seeking for recommendation from it at the same time as you feel down. By reframing your thoughts on this way, you could begin to shift your thoughts faraway from the poor self-speak loop and closer to a more high first-class, answer-focused mindset.

Another technique for combatting terrible self-speak is to exercise mindfulness. Mindfulness is the exercise of taking note of the present moment with out judgment. By running toward mindfulness, you may end up more aware about your mind and feelings and learn how to take a look at them without getting caught up in them. This will will assist you to damage unfastened from the cycle of overthinking and terrible self-talk.

In addition to reframing your mind and practising mindfulness, it is crucial to additionally be type to your self. Treat yourself with the equal kindness and compassion which you could provide a pal. Remember, no person is best, and it is accurate enough to make errors. By being kind to your self, you could lessen strain and anxiety and destroy unfastened from the overthinking lure.

Finally, it may be beneficial to engage in bodily interest or workout to help launch strain and anxiety. Exercise has been hooked up to lessen the symptoms of tension and melancholy and may help damage the cycle of awful self-speak and overthinking. Try going for a walk or run, operating towards yoga, or undertaking every one-of-a-kind physical interest which you experience.

Negative self-speak can also have a profound impact to your mind and behavior, primary to a sample of overthinking. But through using working towards self-compassion, reframing your thoughts, and tasty in mindfulness and bodily interest, you could spoil loose from the overthinking lure and rewire your mind towards positivity and well-being. Give the ones physical sports a try to see how they help you to triumph over overthinking and terrible self-talk.

Chapter 4: How To Stop Overanalyzing And Take Action

Do you find your self suffering to make alternatives? Do you spend hours weighing the specialists and cons, only to turn out to be feeling paralyzed through indecision? If so, you are not on my own. Many humans be troubled with the aid of using the overthinking trap near making choices. But what's it approximately selection-making that makes us so susceptible to overthinking?

One element is the concern of making the incorrect preference. We fear approximately the capacity effects of our alternatives, and this anxiety can reason us to come to be caught in a cycle of overthinking. We additionally can be inspired with the aid of manner of manner of cognitive biases that make us overvalue superb options and undervalue others.

Another issue is the complexity of selection-making. With such numerous variables to recollect, it is clean to get slowed down in assessment paralysis. We also can sense pressure to make the "right" desire, principal us to obsess over each detail and opportunity.

So, how are we able to damage unfastened from the overthinking trap and make alternatives with self assurance? One method is to popularity on our values and priorities. By clarifying what's most crucial to us, we're capable of higher have a look at our options and make selections that align with our desires.

Another technique is to restrict our alternatives. When confronted with too many alternatives, we can also feel overwhelmed and war to select. By narrowing down our alternatives and focusing on the most promising ones, we are capable of simplify the choice-making way and reduce our pressure tiers.

It's additionally beneficial to apprehend at the same time as we're task bad self-speak. The way we talk to ourselves can have a powerful effect on our conduct and feelings. By reframing our mind in a greater top notch and optimistic manner, we're able to overcome self-doubt and assemble our self assurance in choice-making.

To positioned the ones techniques into exercise, try the following exercise:

Make a listing of your values and priorities. What topics maximum to you in lifestyles?

Identify a selection you've got been suffering with. Write down all of the options you've got been considering.

Use your listing of values and priorities to evaluate each possibility. Which alternatives align exceptional with what's important to you?

Narrow down your alternatives to the top or three. Focus on those choices and set a last date for you make a decision.

Chapter 5: Perfectionism: Why Striving For Perfection Can Fuel Overthinking

In a worldwide wherein achievement is regularly equated with perfection, it's far easy to get trapped within the cycle of overthinking. As human beings, every body attempt for excellence, but on the same time as this could become an obsession, it is able to bring about self-doubt and normal rumination. In this monetary wreck, we are able to find out the hyperlink among perfectionism and overthinking, and discover ways to permit circulate of the want for perfection.

Perfectionism is a trait this is frequently praised, however it can have essential consequences for intellectual health. Research suggests that oldsters that are perfectionistic are much more likely to enjoy anxiety, melancholy, and coffee shallowness. The regular pressure to be perfect can gasoline overthinking, due to the fact the mind turns into preoccupied with the concern of failure.

The problem with perfectionism is that it is fantastic. No you could ever be amazing, and the pursuit of perfection can emerge as an limitless cycle of frustration and disappointment. It's vital to recognize that perfectionism is not a healthy way of striving for excellence. In reality, it can save you improvement and limit creativity.

One way to combat perfectionism is to embody imperfection. This may also moreover appear counterintuitive, however accepting that mistakes will manifest and that failure is a natural a part of the reading method can help reduce the pressure to be amazing. This may be tough, specially for people who've an extended information of striving for perfection, but it's miles crucial to bear in mind that imperfection is a part of being human.

Another technique for overcoming perfectionism is to popularity on progress, in location of perfection. This way putting practical goals and celebrating small successes alongside the manner. By moving the point of interest from the give up end result to the method of increase, people can reduce the stress to be perfect and enjoy the adventure.

It's additionally beneficial to venture bad self-speak that frequently accompanies perfectionism. The inner critic may be relentless, and it is critical to recognize while horrible self-communicate is taking up. When thoughts like "I'm now not suitable enough" or "I'll in no way be able to try this flawlessly" arise, it's far useful to project them with evidence to the opposite. For instance, in case you're operating on a project and discover yourself getting stuck in a perfectionistic mind-set, you may remind your self of instances even as you've got efficiently finished similar obligations inside the past.

Finally, it's far critical to workout self-compassion. This manner treating yourself with kindness and know-how, in place of harsh complaint. Remember that everyone makes errors and tales setbacks. It's ok to be imperfect, and getting to know to actually be given yourself flaws and all can be a effective antidote to overthinking.

Make a listing of your top 3 perfectionistic inclinations. Write down how they make contributions for your overthinking and find out how you could shift your mind-set to encompass imperfection.

Practice self-compassion through writing a letter to yourself as in case you had been talking to a pal. Write down phrases of encouragement and compassion, acknowledging that everyone makes mistakes and that it's miles okay to be imperfect.

Chapter 6: The Power Of Gratitude

Do you often discover your self out of place in a sea of issues and horrible mind? Do you struggle to interrupt free from the cycle of overthinking? If so, it's time to turn to the energy of gratitude and brilliant thinking.

Research indicates that cultivating gratitude can also have a profound impact on our intellectual fitness and properly-being. Studies have placed that individuals who frequently exercise gratitude are greater advantageous, revel in more delight and satisfaction, and function lower levels of strain and despair.

But how exactly does gratitude assist us combat overthinking? Let's take a better look.

Gratitude shifts our interest from what is wrong to what is right. When we are stuck in a cycle of horrible thinking, it is straightforward to get caught up in all of the subjects which might be going incorrect in our lives. But via the use of intentionally focusing on the matters we are grateful for, we shift our hobby to the first rate components of our lives.

Gratitude allows us reframe our thoughts. When we're overthinking, it's miles often due to the fact we are caught in awful concept styles. But with the resource of practising gratitude, we're capable of start to reframe our mind and spot subjects from a greater powerful attitude. For example, rather than residing on all the matters that might move incorrect, we can consciousness at the topics which may be going right and sense grateful for them.

Gratitude promotes mindfulness. When we're thankful, we're completely gift within the second and appreciative of what we've got got were given. This mindfulness permits us destroy loose from the cycle of overthinking and attention on the right right here and now.

So how can you cultivate gratitude in your existence? Here are a few sports to get you started out:

Keep a gratitude magazine. Each day, write down three assets you are thankful for. They may be large or small, and they'll be some thing from the people to your lifestyles to the clean pleasures of everyday existence.

Practice gratitude meditation. Take a few minutes each day to take a seat down down in silence and recognition on the property you are thankful for. Visualize these items and permit yourself to revel in grateful for them.

Express your gratitude to others. Take the time to thank the humans in your life who've made a excessive best impact on you. Write a thank-you be conscious, deliver a text, or truly say thank you in individual.

By training gratitude and powerful questioning, you could ruin loose from the cycle of overthinking and cultivate a more great and beautiful lifestyles. Give it a try to see the distinction it can make.

Chapter 7: How To Break Free From Repetitive Thoughts

Rumination, or the tendency to stay on horrific mind or research, can be a not unusual motive of overthinking. This cycle of repetitive thoughts can often enjoy like a lure, leaving us feeling stuck and unable to transport earlier. However, through statistics the technological know-how inside the once more of rumination and learning strategies to break loose from those patterns, we're able to take steps to triumph over overthinking and enhance our trendy properly-being.

One of the important component components of rumination is the manner that it turns on the thoughts's default mode network (DMN). This network is answerable for processing self-referential mind and recollections, that might lead to a cycle of repetitive, horrible thinking. In reality, research has established that folks that commonly have a tendency to ruminate have an overactive DMN, that could reason troubles in regulating feelings and selection-making.

To destroy unfastened from the cycle of rumination, it could be beneficial to workout mindfulness techniques. By that specialize inside the prevailing second and searching at our mind with out judgment, we're capable of begin to disengage from terrible idea patterns and redirect our interest to extra satisfactory reports. Mindfulness sporting events like deep respiration, body scans, and meditation can help us cultivate cognizance of our mind and feelings, and build resilience in the face of difficult situations.

Chapter 8: Cognitive Distortions

Over thinking may be a debilitating addiction that consumes our thoughts and leaves us feeling stuck. It's a vicious cycle of bad thoughts and disturbing that might bring about anxiety, despair, and a famous enjoy of dissatisfaction with lifestyles. However, there are techniques to interrupt loose from this lure and start living a more enjoyable lifestyles.

One of the important thing elements that make contributions to overthinking is cognitive distortions. These are sorts of questioning that are faulty or unhelpful however may be tough to apprehend because of the reality they enjoy so familiar. For example, catastrophizing is a not unusual cognitive distortion that includes imagining the worst viable final results of a scenario. This can result in excessive worry and anxiety, which handiest serves to feed the cycle of overthinking.

To destroy unfastened from cognitive distortions, it is important to start by using the usage of recognizing them. This can contain maintaining a magazine or surely being attentive to your mind throughout the day. When you be conscious a sample of bad thinking, try and assignment it. Ask your self if there is proof to assist this notion or if there are opportunity motives that is probably more correct.

Another beneficial method for preventing overthinking is to exercising mindfulness. This includes being fully present within the 2d, without judgment or distraction. Mindfulness can assist us to interrupt loose from terrible idea patterns and to popularity on what goes on within the present second. This can be particularly beneficial whilst we find out ourselves ruminating on past occasions or traumatic approximately the future.

Gratitude is any other powerful device for preventing overthinking. When we consciousness at the topics we are grateful for, we're plenty much less possibly to get stuck up in horrible questioning styles. Practicing gratitude can include preserving a gratitude mag or actually taking time every day to mirror on the topics we respect in our lives.

Exercise additionally can be an powerful manner to fight overthinking. Exercise releases endorphins, which can be herbal temper-boosters which could help us to revel in greater first-rate and much less annoying. Exercise moreover gives a distraction from terrible thoughts, permitting us to focus on some component else for a while.

Finally, it's miles critical to recollect that breaking unfastened from overthinking is a way. It's now not probable that we can be able to simply remove overthinking from our lives, but we are capable of discover ways to control it greater successfully. By running toward mindfulness, hard our terrible mind, and that specialize in gratitude and exercise, we are able to start to interrupt unfastened from the overthinking lure and stay a greater pleasing lifestyles.

Chapter 9: How To Manage Stress For A Clearer Mind

Stress is a common a part of our lives, however it is able to additionally be a chief contributor to overthinking. When we are pressured, our brains are flooded with cortisol, a hormone which could result in tension and make it tougher to assume simply. This is why it's miles important to learn how to manipulate pressure so you can save you it from fueling overthinking.

One powerful manner to control stress is through rest strategies. Practicing deep respiration sporting activities or revolutionary muscle rest can help calm your mind and frame, making it less difficult to reputation on the prevailing second and permit cross of stressors that can be contributing to overthinking.

Another approach to control stress is thru physical pastime. Exercise releases endorphins, that would increase your mood and decrease feelings of pressure and tension. Whether it's going for a walk or hitting the fitness center, locating an interest that you revel in and that receives your coronary coronary heart price up can be a exquisite way to fight the awful consequences of strain.

In addition to the ones techniques, it's essential to moreover come to be aware about and address the property of strain for your life. This also can contain putting barriers in your relationships or taking steps to manipulate your workload more effectively. By lowering the amount of pressure you enjoy on a every day foundation, you could create a extra conducive surroundings for clean thinking and reduce the threat of getting stuck within the overthinking trap.

Another essential problem of managing pressure is calling after your bodily health. Eating a balanced diet, getting sufficient sleep, and averting bad conduct like smoking or immoderate alcohol consumption can all help reduce pressure stages and promote a clearer thoughts. When your frame is well-cared for, your mind is better geared up to cope with the stressful situations and stressors that lifestyles throws your manner.

Another technique for managing stress and decreasing overthinking is to engage in regular physical interest. Exercise has been shown to have a exquisite impact on intellectual health, which includes decreasing stress and anxiety. This is due to the fact workout releases endorphins, which may be natural sense-accurate chemical substances inside the thoughts. Additionally, exercise can help to easy the mind and offer a revel in of hobby and accomplishment. Try incorporating each day physical hobby into your normal, which include taking a stroll, operating towards yoga, or becoming a member of a sports activities activities sports activities institution.

Another approach for managing pressure and lowering overthinking is to exercising rest techniques. These can consist of deep breathing physical video games, current muscle rest, or visualization strategies. These techniques can help to lessen the physiological signs and symptoms and symptoms of stress, which includes accelerated coronary coronary heart fee and shallow respiration. By running within the course of relaxation techniques often, you may teach your frame to reply to strain in a calmer and greater managed way.

Finally, it's far crucial to prioritize self-care that permits you to govern strain and reduce overthinking. This can embody getting enough sleep, eating a balanced food plan, and attractive in sports activities that deliver you pleasure and rest. It can also embody placing obstacles and announcing no to activities or commitments that can purpose pointless stress or weigh down. By prioritizing self-care, you may improve your chosen well-being and reduce the effect of stress to your existence.

Exercise:

Take a 30-minute stroll out of doors every day.

Join a close-by gym or fitness elegance.

Practice yoga or other aware movement practices.

Relaxation techniques:

Practice deep respiration sports activities for five-10 minutes each day.

Try modern-day muscle relaxation, in which you traumatic and then release each muscle group on your body.

Use visualization techniques to imagine your self in a peaceful environment.

Chapter 10: The Power Of Perspective

We all have a completely unique attitude on the world round us. This angle may want to have a profound effect on how we assume and experience. When it involves overthinking, our mindset can either gasoline the cycle or assist us spoil loose from it. In this financial disaster, we're going to find out the energy of mind-set in reducing overthinking and percentage strategies for transferring your mindset.

First, it's far critical to recognize that our mind-set is long-established with the useful resource of our research, ideals, and values. When we are stuck in a cycle of overthinking, our attitude can come to be slender and distorted. We can also reputation only on the negative factors of a situation, blow subjects out of percent, or catastrophize the destiny. This sort of wondering pleasant serves to perpetuate the cycle of overthinking.

One way to shift your attitude is to exercise mindfulness. Mindfulness includes being attentive to the triumphing second with out judgment. By being sincerely gift and aware of our thoughts and emotions, we are capable of gain a more balanced mind-set. Mindfulness can also help us allow pass of negative thoughts and emotions that can be fueling our overthinking.

Another approach for shifting your perspective is to reframe bad mind. Reframing includes taking a horrible idea and turning it right right into a satisfactory or more impartial idea. For instance, if you're constantly traumatic approximately the future, strive reframing your mind through specializing inside the existing 2nd and the actions you could take to put together for the future.

Gratitude is also a effective device for transferring your mind-set. When we recognition on the good stuff in our lives, it may help us benefit a greater powerful outlook and decrease the cycle of overthinking. Take some time every day to mirror at the things you're grateful for, regardless of how small they may seem.

Finally, it is essential to recognize that our mind-set isn't always steady. We have the electricity to exchange our angle and the manner we keep in mind the arena spherical us. By schooling mindfulness, reframing terrible mind, and cultivating gratitude, we're able to shift our mind-set and reduce the cycle of overthinking.

Here are some bodily video games to help you shift your mind-set:

Mindful respiration: Take a few minutes every day to attention to your breath. Notice the feeling of the breath transferring inner and out of your frame. If your thoughts begins to wander, gently deliver your attention lower back on your breath.

Chapter 11: How To Overcome Analysis Paralysis"

Do you ever feel like you're drowning in a sea of choices? From what to put on within the morning to wherein to move for dinner, every selection appears to end up an countless highbrow loop of overthinking. This is referred to as evaluation paralysis, a phenomenon this is turning into increasingly more common in modern-day speedy-paced society. In this chapter, we can discover the technological know-how in the back of the ambiguity of choice and offer you with strategies to triumph over evaluation paralysis.

The Paradox of Choice:

The paradox of choice is the phenomenon where having too many options can reason tension and choice paralysis. This occurs due to the reality our brains are confused out to are seeking for the extremely good possible final results, and while faced with too many options, we war to decide the excellent one.

According to a have a take a look at performed with the aid of Sheena Iyengar, a professor of control at Columbia University, humans are more likely to make a purchase at the equal time as provided with a limited range of alternatives, in choice to an first-rate preference. Therefore, it's far crucial to restrict the amount of alternatives available to reduce assessment paralysis.

The Art of Letting Go:

Letting flow is one of the most hard elements of overcoming assessment paralysis. We often maintain onto a preference, seeking out to nice it, and grow to be overthinking it to the factor of exhaustion. One technique to combat that is to exercise mindfulness. By being present in the 2d, we're able to famend our thoughts and allow them to move. Mindfulness also enables us to advantage attitude, permitting us to peer the larger photograph, that can provide readability at the same time as making options.

The Power of Visualization:

Visualization is a powerful tool that could assist triumph over evaluation paralysis. When we visualize a choice, we are more likely to feel confident and devoted to our choice. This technique is substantially applied in sports sports psychology, in which athletes visualize themselves efficaciously completing a particular glide or maneuver. You can exercise this technique with the useful aid of visualizing yourself you make a decision and feeling assured in it. This workout will help to lessen anxiety and offer readability while making picks.

The Importance of Time:

Time is a critical aspect even as making alternatives. When we're rushed, we have a propensity to make hasty choices that won't be well perception out. On the opposite hand, whilst we have too much time, we normally commonly have a tendency to overthink, important to assessment paralysis. Therefore, it is crucial to set deadlines for choice-making. This will assist to provide a experience of urgency and save you overthinking. Additionally, breaking down huge alternatives into smaller, extra plausible steps can help to simplify the system and decrease the feeling of being crushed.

Analysis paralysis is a commonplace problem in present day-day society. However, with the resource of the usage of proscribing choices, practicing mindfulness, using visualization techniques, setting ultimate dates, and breaking down large decisions, you may conquer evaluation paralysis. Remember, it's miles vital to reputation on the larger photo, accept as true with your instincts, and do no longer be afraid to make errors. By embracing those strategies, you can emerge as a more assured selection-maker and conquer the ambiguity of choice.

Chapter 12: How To Release Negative Thoughts And Embrace Change

Overthinking can often be fueled by way of manner of our attachment to bad thoughts and feelings, leading to a in no manner-completing cycle of rumination. However, the art work of letting flow can assist us damage loose from this cycle and consist of alternate.

Letting skip way accepting that we can not control everything in our lives, which incorporates our mind and emotions. It method spotting that retaining onto horrific mind excellent motives us extra suffering and stops us from transferring beforehand. By freeing those mind and feelings, we create region for logo spanking new, brilliant testimonies and a more match mind-set.

To start working towards the art of letting go, it is crucial to first renowned the thoughts and emotions that are causing us misery. This may additionally comprise journaling or talking with a therapist or depended on pal. Once we've got identified those mind and emotions, we're capable of begin to project them and reframe them in a extra great light.

One effective workout for letting flow is the "perception stopping" method. When a negative belief arises, in reality say "prevent" or "cancel" out loud and visualize the concept disappearing. Then, update the horrific idea with a super confirmation or picture. This approach allows to interrupt the cycle of overthinking and rewire our thoughts to recognition on more powerful thoughts.

Another technique for letting pass is mindfulness meditation. By working inside the path of mindfulness, we learn how to test our mind without judgment and allow them to pass with out becoming connected to them. This permits us to boom a more balanced mind-set and decrease our tendency to ruminate.

Letting pass additionally includes embracing alternate and accepting that it is a natural a part of life. When we withstand exchange, we create greater pressure and tension for ourselves. By embracing alternate, we open ourselves as a whole lot as new possibilities and reports, that could help us develop and increase in tremendous strategies.

To practice embracing trade, try doing some thing new or one of a kind every day. This may be as clean as attempting a ultra-modern meals or taking a incredible path to paintings. By exposing ourselves to new research, we end up more comfortable with exchange and additional adaptable to new conditions.

Ultimately, the artwork of letting bypass calls for us to cultivate self-compassion and forgiveness. We should learn how to forgive ourselves for our mistakes and allow cross of any shame or guilt we can be carrying. By doing so, we unfastened ourselves from the load of our past and permit ourselves to move beforehand with a lighter coronary heart and clearer thoughts.

Chapter 13: How To Improve Your Sleep Habits For A Clearer Mind

Sleep is one of the most essential additives of our not unusual health and nicely-being. It permits our frame to rest and recharge, selling pinnacle-satisfactory physical and mental functioning. However, for lots people, getting enough first-class sleep may be tough, essential to an overactive and overthinking thoughts. In this bankruptcy, we are able to find out the era of sleep, the way it influences overthinking, and percentage realistic physical games for enhancing your sleep behavior.

Our frame's herbal sleep cycle is regulated via the use of a complex network of biological strategies, together with hormones and neurotransmitters. These strategies manipulate while we enjoy sleepy or alert, and the period and satisfactory of our sleep. However, numerous elements can disrupt our herbal sleep cycle, which incorporates pressure, anxiety, and bad sleep conduct.

One of the maximum huge affects of sleep deprivation is an overactive mind. When we do no longer get sufficient sleep, our brains turn out to be overstimulated, essential to problem in interest and improved tension. This can then bring about a cycle of overthinking, which similarly interferes with our capability to nod off and live asleep.

Fortunately, there are numerous steps you can take to enhance your sleep conduct and reduce overthinking. Firstly, try to installation a consistent sleep time table with the aid of going to mattress and waking up at the same time every day. This helps to regulate your frame's inner clock and sell higher superb sleep.

It's also vital to create a calming environment for your bed room. This technique casting off any distractions together with electronics, retaining the room cool and darkish, and the usage of cushty bedding. This will help sign in your mind that it's time to wind down and get ready for sleep.

Another important difficulty in selling higher sleep is decreasing stress and tension. Practice relaxation strategies which embody deep respiration, meditation, or yoga to help calm your thoughts and promote relaxation. Additionally, avoid stimulating sports activities sports together with using electronics or exercising close to bedtime.

One of the most commonplace sleep issues is insomnia, characterized via problem falling asleep or staying asleep. If you battle with insomnia, strive incorporating cognitive-behavioral treatment (CBT) techniques, which will let you choose out out and mission horrible thoughts that can be contributing in your sleep issues.

In addition to way of life modifications, numerous herbal remedies can sell better sleep. These include herbal nutritional dietary supplements together with valerian root or chamomile, which have been confirmed to have a relaxing impact on the body. Additionally, some essential oils which incorporates lavender or bergamot may be used to promote relaxation and reduce anxiety.

Sleep is a crucial thing of lowering overthinking and selling greatest mental and physical health. By adopting healthful sleep conduct and making manner of life changes, you may beautify your sleep splendid and decrease the effect of overthinking in your each day life. Remember, small modifications need to have a big impact, so begin in recent times thru manner of implementing one or of these recommendations and watch your sleep behavior and overthinking decorate over the years.

Chapter 14: The Role Of Exercise In Reducing Over Thinking

Overthinking can be a chronic and tough dependancy to interrupt. It's clean to get caught up in repetitive mind, reading each decision and movement until you experience paralyzed via indecision. But did that exercising may be an powerful way to fight overthinking? In this financial ruin, we're going to explore the technology inside the once more of the way exercising can help lessen overthinking, and provide sensible tips for incorporating physical interest into your each day normal.

First, allow's take a better observe the relationship amongst exercising and overthinking. Research has tested that ordinary exercising can lessen symptoms of anxiety and despair, conditions often associated with overthinking. Exercise will increase the producing of endorphins, neurotransmitters that can enhance temper and reduce strain degrees. It also can boom the discharge of mind-derived neurotrophic component (BDNF), a protein that performs a feature in neuroplasticity, the mind's capability to comply and change in reaction to new tales.

Incorporating physical pastime into your every day everyday also can offer a enjoy of structure and routine, which could help alleviate feelings of weigh down and tension that often accompany overthinking. Exercise can also offer a revel in of feat and self-efficacy, boosting shallowness and self warranty to your capability to cope with strain and disturbing situations.

So, how can you incorporate exercise into your every day recurring to lessen overthinking? Here are some suggestions:

Start small: If you are new to exercise, it is important to begin small and step by step growth the intensity and length of your sports. This will assist prevent damage and make sure that workout is a sustainable a part of your ordinary. Even a brief stroll or moderate stretching can be beneficial in reducing strain and improving mood.

Find an interest you revel in: It's masses easier to paste to a exercising normal if you enjoy the hobby you're doing. Experiment with wonderful styles of exercise, at the side of yoga, on foot, swimming, or cycling, until you discover some factor that feels fun and profitable.

Set sensible goals: Setting sensible dreams permit you to stay inspired and focused at the blessings of workout. Whether it is aiming to stroll for 30 minutes a day or taking walks a 5K, putting viable desires let you gather momentum and sense a revel in of success.

Incorporate motion into your every day routine: You do now not should hit the health club to collect the advantages of workout. Finding tactics to encompass movement into your each day ordinary, on the side of taking the steps in preference to the elevator or going for a walk in the course of your lunch harm, can be a smooth and effective way to enhance your temper and reduce overthinking.

Make exercising a social hobby: Exercising with buddies or turning into a member of a set fitness beauty can provide a revel in of network and resource, making it less complicated to paste to your routine and stay motivated.

In addition to the ones practical hints, it's far essential to method exercising with a mind-set of self-compassion and popularity. Remember that exercise isn't a magic treatment for overthinking, and it is adequate to have days even as you do no longer experience as lots as running out. By cultivating a sense of self-compassion and recognition, you can keep away from falling into the trap of perfectionism and permit your self to acquire the benefits of workout with out which include useless pressure or pressure.

Chapter 15: How To Eat For A Clearer Mind

Overthinking may be a hard problem to overcome, mainly whilst it appears to devour every idea and movement. While there are various techniques and strategies to manipulate overthinking, one location this is often neglected is vitamins. The meals we devour should have a huge impact on our highbrow fitness and cognitive functioning. In this monetary catastrophe, we are able to discover the relationship amongst nutrients and overthinking, and provide pointers for consuming a thoughts-wholesome healthy dietweight-reduction plan.

The Power of Nutrients:

Have you ever observed that your mood can shift counting on what you devour? It appears that the vitamins in our meals may have a profound impact on our mind chemistry. For instance, omega-3 fatty acids, which might be observed in fatty fish, walnuts, and flaxseed, have been tested to reduce contamination in the mind and decorate cognitive characteristic. Similarly, B nutrients, which is probably located in complete grains, leafy greens, and nuts, are vital for wholesome mind function and temper regulation. By ingesting a weight loss program rich in the ones and other thoughts-boosting nutrients, you can decorate your highbrow readability and decrease overthinking.

The Dangers of Processed Foods:

While a few additives can decorate our thoughts feature, others can do the opposite. Processed meals, which might be excessive in sugar, salt, and dangerous fats, have been associated with quite a number of highbrow fitness troubles, in conjunction with anxiety and depression. When we devour processed meals, our blood sugar spikes, decided via a crash, which can motive emotions of irritability and mind fog. In contrast, complete meals, which embody fruits, greens, and lean proteins, offer sustained power and essential nutrients that manual highbrow clarity and normal fitness.

The Importance of Hydration:

Did you recognize that dehydration can impair cognitive characteristic? When we do not drink sufficient water, our mind cells lessen, which could result in fatigue, headaches, and problem concentrating. To live hydrated, purpose to drink at least 8 glasses of water in keeping with day, and keep away from sugary liquids, that could dehydrate the frame even further. Additionally, incorporating ingredients with high water content material, which includes watermelon, cucumber, and celery, will let you live hydrated and decorate intellectual readability.

Mindful Eating:

Have you ever decided your self ingesting with out even considering what you are putting in your mouth? Mindless ingesting can reason overconsumption and horrific meals picks, that would have bad effects on our highbrow fitness. By running toward conscious ingesting, we're capable of cultivate a deeper reputation of our food selections and how they make us sense. This involves being attentive to our starvation and fullness cues, savoring the flavors and textures of our meals, and keeping off distractions whilst eating. By training conscious consuming, we are capable of make better food alternatives and decorate our intellectual readability.

Practical Exercises:

Keep a food mag: For one week, document the whole lot you devour and drink, along side the manner it makes you enjoy. This will assist you choose out patterns and make adjustments to your healthy eating plan as favored.

Swap out processed meals: Try converting one processed meals object on your eating regimen with a whole food possibility. For instance, exchange out chips for carrot sticks, or sugary drinks for water or natural tea.

Experiment with mind-boosting meals: Incorporate extra components which can be immoderate in mind-boosting nutrients, such as fatty fish, nuts, and leafy veggies, into your weight-reduction plan. Try new recipes and experiment with unique flavors and textures.

By making easy changes to our food regimen, we can enhance our highbrow clarity and reduce overthinking. By incorporating thoughts-boosting nutrients, averting processed meals, staying hydrated, and practising aware ingesting, we will nourish our minds and our bodies and domesticate a enjoy of balance and calm. So the following time you discover yourself stuck in a cycle of overthinking, don't forget reaching for a mind-wholesome snack.

Chapter 16: The Power Of Creativity

Do you ever locate yourself out of place in concept, ad infinitum reading a scenario or replaying a verbal exchange to your thoughts? Overthinking may be a debilitating cycle that drains your energy and makes it hard to take action. However, there's a effective tool that would assist damage this cycle: creativity. In this financial disaster, we can discover the generation within the once more of the relationship amongst creativity and overthinking, and offer strategies and sports for harnessing your creativeness to lessen overthinking.

First, allow's discover why creativity may be this kind of powerful device in lowering overthinking. When we've got interplay in modern sports, our minds are targeted on the prevailing 2d, which allows us to interrupt free from the limitless cycle of overthinking. Furthermore, creativity affords an outlet for our thoughts and emotions, permitting us to specific ourselves and launch pent-up strain and anxiety. In fact, research have established that assignment progressive sports which includes writing, drawing, or playing track can lessen symptoms of tension and depression.

One approach for harnessing the strength of creativity to lessen overthinking is journaling. Writing down your mind and feelings can assist to release them from your thoughts, providing you with a smooth attitude and decreasing the intensity of your emotions. To get commenced, set aside a while each day to write down down down your mind and feelings with out judgement. Allow your self to put in writing down freely, with out annoying about grammar or spelling. This can be a effective way to launch pent-up feelings and reduce the intensity of your overthinking.

Another approach for harnessing the strength of creativity is visualization. Visualization is the method of the usage of your creativeness to create highbrow pics or conditions. When we visualize a superb very last consequences, it can assist to reduce feelings of hysteria and growth our self warranty and motivation. To workout visualization, find a quiet space in which you could loosen up and cognizance to your respiratory. Then, visualize your self succeeding in a selected motive or overcoming a selected mission. Allow yourself to absolutely immerse inside the intellectual picture and enjoy the powerful emotions related to it.

Finally, one of the most powerful strategies to harness the power of creativity to reduce overthinking is through modern expression. Whether it's far writing, drawing, painting, or gambling music, conducting progressive sports activities can assist to release pent-up stress and anxiety, and provide a enjoy of purpose and accomplishment. So, in case you're feeling caught in a cycle of overthinking, attempt placing aside a while each day to engage in a progressive interest that you revel in.

Chapter 17: How To Build Relationships That Help Combat Overthinking

Overthinking can be a hard trouble to triumph over, mainly even as it appears to eat each perception and movement. While there are numerous techniques and techniques to manage overthinking, one region this is regularly overlooked is social useful aid. Building sturdy relationships with others can provide a experience of comfort and validation, and might help fight feelings of loneliness and isolation. In this financial spoil, we will find out the significance of social manual in reducing overthinking and provide hints for constructing relationships that resource highbrow fitness.

The Power of Social Connection:

Humans are social creatures through nature, and our connections with others ought to have a profound impact on our highbrow fitness. In reality, studies has proven that social assistance is a big predictor of nicely-being, and can guard in opposition to intellectual health troubles inclusive of despair and anxiety. By building robust relationships with others, we're capable of benefit a experience of belonging and validation that could assist fight emotions of loneliness and isolation.

The Importance of Vulnerability:

Building strong relationships requires vulnerability, which can be hard for those struggling with overthinking. Vulnerability consists of starting as a good buy as others and sharing our mind and feelings, even when it feels uncomfortable or horrifying. However, via schooling vulnerability, we will construct deeper connections with others and advantage a feel of validation and guide. It's important to keep in thoughts that vulnerability is a -way street, and with the aid of the usage of being willing with others, we create a space for them to be willing with us.

The Role of Boundaries:

While constructing sturdy relationships is important, it is in addition vital to set limitations that guard our highbrow fitness. Boundaries are limits that we set for ourselves and others to ensure that our wishes are being met and that we are not being taken advantage of. By putting limitations, we can communicate our desires to others and protect ourselves from risky relationships. It's essential to do not forget that boundaries are not selfish, but as a substitute a important shape of self-care.

Practical Exercises:

Reach out to a chum: Take the time to reach out to a friend or cherished one that you have not talked to in a while. Ask them how they may be doing and share how you are feeling.

Practice vulnerability: Pick one person on your lifestyles which you agree with and workout vulnerability with them. Share a few aspect which you've been struggling with and ask for their help.

Set a boundary: Identify a place of your lifestyles in which you need to set a boundary. Communicate this boundary to the ones spherical you and stay with it.

Building strong relationships with others is a crucial factor of dealing with overthinking and maintaining suitable highbrow health. By working towards vulnerability, placing limitations, and reaching out to others, we are capable of construct significant connections that provide a revel in of validation and manual. So the following time you find out your self suffering with overthinking, hold in thoughts achieving out to a person you take delivery of as real with and constructing a relationship that enables your intellectual health.

Chapter 18: The Benefits Of Laughter: How To Use Humor To Combat Overthinking

Laughter is regularly referred to as the pleasant remedy, and for remarkable purpose. Research has confirmed that laughter has numerous remarkable consequences on each bodily and highbrow health. In truth, laughing has been found to launch endorphins, reduce pressure hormones, enhance the immune tool, or maybe lower ache levels. But what approximately its impact on overthinking? Can laughter in reality assist fight this not unusual problem? The answer is effective, and in this financial disaster, we can discover the benefits of laughter and the manner you could use humor to reduce overthinking.

Firstly, it's far essential to recognize the era at the back of laughter. When we laugh, our mind releases endorphins, which can be chemical materials that promote emotions of satisfaction and properly-being. This can assist to reduce pressure, tension, or perhaps bodily ache. Additionally, laughing will increase blood waft and oxygenation, that would help to decorate cognitive function and memory. These physical outcomes of laughter can assist to create a extra exceptional mind-set, which may be useful in decreasing overthinking.

Another way that laughter can help lessen overthinking is through using growing a enjoy of connection and social help. Laughing with others can help to foster a enjoy of community and belonging, which can be crucial for mental fitness. When we feel supported and related to others, we are more likely to feel wonderful and plenty much less probably to ruminate on bad mind.

So, how can you include laughter and humor into your existence to fight overthinking? One way is to are looking for humorous and uplifting content cloth, inclusive of comedy suggests, funny podcasts, or funny books. Watching a funny movie or TV show with pals or circle of relatives additionally may be a extraordinary way to bond and relieve strain.

Additionally, locating techniques to include humor into your every day existence can be useful. This might also moreover need to suggest creating a aware attempt to locate the humor in regular conditions, or perhaps finding procedures to playfully tease your self even as you be aware that you are overthinking. By reframing awful mind with humor, you can create a greater splendid mind-set and reduce the effect of overthinking.

Finally, it is well really worth noting that humor and laughter can be especially useful in conditions in which you may be experiencing anxiety or pressure. In those situations, laughter can offer a miles-wished ruin from horrible thoughts and assist you to technique the situation from a more snug and excellent mindset.

To contain humor and laughter into your each day recurring, attempt some of those bodily sports:

Watch a comedy display or movie: Choose something that you locate especially funny and invite some buddies over to look at it with you.

Find a funny podcast: There are many podcasts that target humor and comedy. Find one which you experience and be aware of it on your journey or for the duration of your downtime.

Play a endeavor: Games which includes Cards Against Humanity or Pictionary may be a fun manner to include humor and laughter into your social existence.

Chapter 19: How To Use Mindfulness Techniques To Reduce Overthinking"

We have a splendid capacity for concept. Our minds are constantly racing, reading, and questioning. However, this tendency inside the course of overthinking also can be damaging to our highbrow and physical fitness. Fortunately, there may be a effective tool that would assist us reduce overthinking and discover extra peace and balance in our lives: mindfulness.

But what exactly is mindfulness, and the way can it help us lessen overthinking? At its middle, mindfulness is a shape of meditation that includes listening to the triumphing 2d with out judgment. By focusing our attention on the existing, we are capable of educate our minds to grow to be more aware about our mind and feelings, and to expand a more enjoy of manage over our highbrow country.

One of the most tremendous advantages of mindfulness is its capability to reduce strain and anxiety. When we overthink, we regularly emerge as stuck up in issues and fears approximately the future. By studying to popularity our interest on the prevailing 2nd, we're capable of ruin loose from this cycle of rumination and discover a more sense of calm and relaxation.

To begin training mindfulness, attempt putting aside a couple of minutes each day to sit down quietly and focus in your breath. Pay interest to the sensation of the air transferring internal and out of your lungs, and try and allow pass of any mind or distractions that get up. Over time, you may find out that this easy exercising permits to reduce your stylish diploma of hysteria and promote a more sense of nicely-being.

Another powerful technique for decreasing overthinking is visualization. By the usage of the electricity of our imagination, we're able to create highbrow snap shots that assist us to interest our mind and feelings. For example, you might imagine your self floating on a non violent, non violent river, or visualizing a shiny, shining slight that envelops and protects you.

To get commenced with visualization, find out a quiet, comfortable location wherein you could sit down or lie down with out distraction. Close your eyes and consciousness for your breath for a few minutes to quiet your thoughts. Then, begin to visualize a chilled image or scene that resonates with you. Allow your self to completely immerse inside the experience and revel in the great feelings that come with it.

In addition to mindfulness and visualization, there are some of extraordinary strategies that could assist to lessen overthinking and promote extra intellectual and bodily fitness. For instance, workout has been confirmed to have a effective effect on the thoughts-body connection, with normal physical hobby supporting to lessen stress and enhance mood.

Similarly, education gratitude also can be a effective tool for decreasing overthinking and selling greater happiness and nicely-being. By focusing on the splendid elements of our lives, we're capable of shift our interest a ways from horrible mind and feelings, and domesticate a extra feel of contentment and peace.

To practice gratitude, strive placing aside a few minutes every day to reflect at the subjects which you are thankful for. This may additionally encompass cherished ones, correct fitness, a cushty domestic, or each different tremendous elements of your lifestyles that you respect. Over time, you can discover that this easy exercising permits to lessen your number one diploma of stress and anxiety, and promotes a more feel of happiness and nicely-being.

Chapter 20: How To Use Positive Self-Talk To Overcome Overthinking"

Overthinking may be a tough dependancy to break, however it is possible. One tool that can be particularly useful in overcoming overthinking is high-quality affirmations.

Positive affirmations are statements that you repeat to yourself regularly to assist red meat up high-quality beliefs and counteract poor self-talk. They can assist shift your thoughts-set from one of self-doubt to 1 in each of self guarantee and self-love. But, are powerful affirmations really a few different form of wishful questioning, or is there generation behind their effectiveness?

Research has validated that fine affirmations can definitely alternate the manner you watched and experience approximately your self. In a check posted within the magazine Social Cognitive and Affective Neuroscience, researchers located that individuals who practiced self-affirmations showed stepped forward interest inside the regions of the mind associated with top notch self confidence and reduced interest within the areas related to horrible self-worth.

So, how can you embody tremendous affirmations into your life to fight overthinking?

One way is to start via identifying the horrible thoughts which can be contributing to your overthinking. These is probably thoughts like "I'm now not properly sufficient" or "I'll in no manner be able to try this." Once you have were given diagnosed those mind, create a list of notable affirmations that straight away counteract them. For example, if your poor idea is "I'm no longer suitable sufficient," your notable confirmation is probably "I am capable and deserving of success."

Repeat these powerful affirmations to yourself each day, both within the morning or earlier than mattress, or maybe at some level in the day while you seize yourself conducting horrible self-communicate. The more you repeat those affirmations, the extra they may become a part of your unconscious thoughts, assisting to shift your simple mind-set towards positivity and self-popularity.

In addition to repeating effective affirmations, it's also important to apply language that supports and empowers you. Instead of the use of terrible language, which includes "I can't" or "I may not," strive using more exceptional language, along side "I can" or "I will." This small shift in language need to make a huge effect for your popular mind-set and assist you conquer overthinking.

Another useful technique is to visualize yourself assignment your dreams and succeeding within the areas in which you commonly generally tend to overthink. Visualization permit you to create a exceptional intellectual photo of yourself and help manual exceptional ideals about your skills. When you visualize yourself succeeding, you're moreover growing a pleasant emotional experience that would assist counteract terrible feelings and reduce overthinking.

To contain visualization into your habitual, take some time each day to anticipate yourself reaching your dreams. Close your eyes and visualize your self in a particular situation, alongside side giving a successful presentation or completing a tough mission. Try to engage all of your senses, imagining what you may see, pay interest, and revel in in that 2nd. The greater vibrant and special you could make your visualization, the more powerful it is going to be.

Lastly, it's miles crucial to hold in thoughts that effective affirmations and amazing strategies aren't a short restoration for overthinking. Breaking terrible thinking styles takes time and effort. But with regular exercising, you can learn how to use remarkable self-speak and visualization to shift your mindset and reduce overthinking.

Incorporating best affirmations and exquisite techniques into your each day regular takes exercise, but the benefits are well well well really worth it. By changing your questioning styles, you can beautify your traditional intellectual fitness, lessen stress and tension, and live a greater exciting existence. So, why now not begin these days? Begin with the aid of identifying the terrible thoughts which can be keeping you once more, and create first-rate affirmations to counteract them. With effort and time, you may harness the electricity of excellent self-talk to triumph over overthinking.

Chapter 21: Understanding Stress

Stress is defined as a country of worry or intellectual tension due to a hard scenario.

The contemporary-day international is a quick-paced and traumatic one. With such a number of wants to some time, it's miles smooth to experience beaten and stressed. Too plenty stress might also additionally have a negative effect on your intellectual and physical fitness, and it is able to even purpose chronic sicknesses.

It's essential to govern strain degrees to live healthy.

Causes of stress:

1. Financial troubles:

Money issues can stem from a fear of not having sufficient, being in debt, or in reality not expertise what the future holds.

2. Relationship problems:

Be it together with your family, friends or accomplice, if a dating is hard, it can be traumatic to be stuck inside the center of it.

three. Job pressure:

Constantly scuffling with collectively together with your boss or co-people can be annoying. Similarly, now not having a project or no longer being glad collectively along with your machine can also motive pressure.

four. Health issues:

Dealing with extreme health issues affecting your bodily nicely- being can also placed strain for your thoughts.

five. Community issues:

If there can be violence on your network or for a few cause you're pressured to depart your own home, it can grow to be a motive of stress.

6. Past regrets and uncertainty approximately the destiny:

Oftentimes people locate it hard to permit bypass in their beyond and awareness on the triumphing. These thoughts additionally result in overthinking approximately the future. The worry of the unknown future can reason intellectual stress.

Feeling a touch little bit of strain at times is ordinary. Everyone opinions it, but excessive strain stages may additionally have an impact for your physical fitness.

Effects of stress:

1. Change in urge for food:

Stress can reason lack of urge for meals or feeling of immoderate hunger. Many humans can not eat while they're experiencing stress, for that reason they turn out to be depleting their our bodies of the vitamins. Contrary to this, a few humans have a propensity to overeat at some stage in stressful situations, predominant to bad consuming behavior.

2. Headaches and frame ache:

Stress can reason bouts of complications or chronic headaches. Some experience frame pain because of intellectual stress. It is crucial to are looking for advice from a doctor if you are experiencing those signs and symptoms.

three. Tightness in chest:

People regularly experience tightness of their chest and hassle in respiration even as the pressure stages are excessive.

four. Fever:

Many revel in a upward thrust in body temperature with boom in intellectual stress degrees.

Apart from physical signs, human beings frequently phrase a alternate in their behaviour.

1. Unable to interest:

Rise in strain degrees is often related to reduced interest tiers. This may be some thing from studies, work, to being attentive to a conversation.

2. Increase irritability:

People have a tendency to get angrier as their pressure will growth. They often discover it difficult to sit down quietly in a single place and are continuously transferring.

three. Insomnia:

Many revel in the incapacity to go to sleep with pressure. This inturn will increase the pressure degrees further.

four. Feeling tired:

Mental pressure can cause the sensation of tiredness. It may be due to alternate in urge for meals, loss of sleep, or every.

five. Unable to govern emotions:

People go through immoderate mood swings from being indignant to being sad or accountable as their strain ranges increase.

Such feelings and emotions are regular even as they may be short-lived. The hassle arises at the same time as you are no longer able to loose your self from this trap.

Stress Response:

Human frame reacts to pressure in a positive manner, flight, fight, or freeze.

All the responses to pressure are this sort of 3. The reaction can trade based completely totally on present day or beyond evaluations, but it's going to usually be in reality one in every of three responses.

Example:

When humans see a snake, they both run, it in reality is flight or stand as a substitute nevertheless it simply is freeze. Whereas a snake handler has been educated for such a situation, they will seize the snake and placed it in a bag, it without a doubt is fight.

Chapter 22: What Is A Stress Trap?

Stress entice is when you can't shake off the feeling of fear or tension, in any other case you again and again discover yourself thinking about a scenario.

Example:

One 2nd you take element in lifestyles, and the following second you are burdened about life.

When you experience a trade to your behaviour no matter the state of affairs, it's far a sign of stress trap.

It's critical to free yourself from this entice and not provide into the ones feelings.

In the approaching chapters, we are able to talk a way to come to be aware about pressure factors and release your self from its entice.

Chapter 23: Engaging

In college instructors ask college college students to pay attention to investigate, and now not distractions. But one manner or the opposite maximum university college students control to do the alternative.

Why is listening to distractions easy?

Because maximum college students are already distracted earlier than the beauty even begins offevolved. Listening to the lecture ought to imply appearing a state-of-the-art activity that they fail to do.

Many people irrespective of their age, reputation, or profession have some factor to fear about. Whenever you try to interest on some difficulty you need to do, the worrisome mind pull you out of your interest. Not being able to provide attention to some detail increases stress.

It's crucial to research the manner to tug yourself out of stressful mind.

No Best Days:

One of the worst topics the area teaches absolutely everyone is 'that is the fine time of your life. If you don't do some thing now, you could pass over out on life's high-quality pleasures'. The time frame of this 'first-rate time to your lifestyles' varies from u.S. To u.S.A. Of america, however it's miles by way of the usage of and massive spherical teenage to early twenties.

The titles 'millionaire at sixteen, eighteen, twenty' and so forth are hobby grabbing and sound pretty correct, but it'd no longer prevent there. Most people have a look at those headlines and suppose they will be insufficient. Though on ground these memories sound inspiring, there may be more to it than meets the eyes.

Studies have verified that nearly eighty% athletes, really millionaires at a young age, pass bankrupt or face financial pressure within five years of retirement. Same is the case with millionaires in the entertainment enterprise. Many of them skip bankrupt irrespective of the paintings they set up.

Some of the well-known names which have long long past bankrupt are Mike Tyson, Lionel Messi, Michael Jackson, and plenty of extra.

Most of those human beings have labored difficult of their young adults to make tens of thousands and thousands, they have long beyond to activities, travelled the arena, enjoyed lifestyles of their teens, however they may be broke of their thirties or forties. They are struggling to discover the money for a tremendous way of life.

On the opportunity hand, maximum human beings with ordinary jobs who can't control to pay for the ones luxuries have enough to stay a fantastic lifestyles even after retirement.

Which facet need to you want to be?

There isn't any such issue as 'the exceptional time'. You can do something you need whenever you want. The incredible instance of this is the founder of Alibaba, Jack Ma, who've become a billionaire after 35 years of age. He has also been a part of the amusement organization after 50 years of age.

The time is now, that is it. You can perform a little component you need, you could collect something you desire at any age.

Stop wondering it is too past due. As prolonged as you're alive, you've got got sufficient time to gain your goals.

Killing the ones horrible mind is essential to alleviate pressure. Whenever you experience out of area to your horrible feelings, try to reconnect together with your surroundings.

Reconnect:

How to reconnect?

It's smooth in current-day day speedy-paced life to be disconnected with the arena round you.

Slow down. Look spherical at the 5 gadgets you can see. Notice their form, their characteristic, their shadows. Breath in the air slowly. Notice the way it smells. Reach out and experience the devices spherical you. Notice their texture, temperature. Listen to the sounds. How many sounds are you capable of pay attention? Notice the taste on your mouth.

Example:

If you're consuming some issue, be conscious the taste of that drink however the reality that it's far water.

If you are spending time with a person, refocus your attention on what they are announcing, word their expressions, the tone of their voice, the pitch.

If you are studying a few issue and enjoy distracted, have a look at the three sentences out loud, registering every single phrase. This manner you may be capable of bring your hobby decrease decrease again on your studying fabric.

Every time you get distracted by way of manner of demanding mind, workout reconnecting at the side of your surroundings. The extra you do it, the quicker you'll learn how to reconnect collectively along with your international. Try to training this exercise ordinary.

Inner hurricane:

Sometimes irrespective of how tough you attempt, you fail to recognition for your surroundings. The storm of your thoughts can be overwhelming and reconnecting can be tough in the path of such events.

When you feel such as you cannot prevent your terrible internal mind, do that exercise.

Focus for your breaths. Exhale clearly, emptying your lungs, pause for 3 seconds earlier than inhaling. Inhale as slowly as you can. Take in shallow breaths, no longer deep breaths. If you feel lightheaded, you are respiratory too fast or too deep. Slow down. Pay hobby in your respiratory. Notice the waft of air via your nostrils, the upward push and fall of your shoulders, and the outside and inside actions of your stomach.

Place your toes in opposition to the floor and upward push up. Notice the feel of the floor. Stretch your arms slowly or press them collectively.

Now take a look at your surroundings. Note 5 items you can see. Reconnect with the region around you. Listen to the sounds, be aware the smells, touch the gadgets and join up the way it feels.

Whenever annoying mind appear, reconnect and have interaction with the world spherical you.

These physical video games will not get rid of your stress completely, however they'll assist you cope with the terrible thoughts.

To take away stress, you may want to put off the idea reason. Everyone is burdened due to fantastic motives. Try to find out your reason and art work on it.

Like any new functionality, these bodily games may be difficult to observe in the beginning. The more you preparation them, the less difficult they may get.

Stop Overthinking

The Paralysis of Analysis:

Have you ever located yourself caught in a loop of overthinking and analysing every preference you're making? This is a common trouble that many human beings face, called the 'paralysis of evaluation'. It can arise in loads of various strategies, from obsessing over small data to continuously 2nd-guessing your alternatives.

Understanding Overthinking and How It Affects Your Life

Overthinking, furthermore referred to as the paralysis of evaluation, is a common problem that can have an effect on every person from all walks of life. It's a belief technique that involves residing on a particular hassle, situation or selection to such an extent that it becomes tough to make any improvement. Overthinking may be debilitating and might save you you from making essential selections, taking critical movements, and gambling the prevailing 2d.

The problem with overthinking is that it is able to result in a vicious cycle that is difficult to break. The extra you keep in mind a hassle, the greater you emerge as enthusiastic about finding a solution, and the more you end up crushed via the use of the complexity of the scenario. This can reason emotions of anxiety, strain, and depression, which best serve to compound the trouble.

There are many motives why humans overthink. For some, it can be a coping mechanism for tension or pressure. For others, it can be a addiction that superior over time. In specific times, it may be a end give up result of perfectionism, wherein the concern of making errors or failure can cause over analysing and overthinking.

Overthinking may additionally have a profound impact on intellectual health, inflicting tension, melancholy, and different highbrow fitness troubles. When you overthink, your minds grow to be consumed with a unmarried concept, concept, or problem. This may be dangerous, as it may result in a cycle of terrible wondering and rumination, that can reason your highbrow fitness to go to pot over time.

In some times, overthinking may additionally even motive bodily health problems, including headaches, insomnia, and fatigue. The regular fear and pressure that include overthinking can take a toll on your body, making it tough to feature every mentally and bodily.

This should make it tough to talk effectively with others, and might even bring about misunderstandings and war.

It can also cause you to withdraw from social conditions, as you could experience too self-aware or concerned approximately how others understand you. This can result in emotions of loneliness and isolation, and might even bring about the dearth of friendships or one-of-a-kind relationships.

Additionally, overthinking can purpose you to hold grudges or resentments, as you could reside at the past mistakes. This ought to make it hard to forgive others or bypass on from terrible reviews, that would further pressure circle of relatives individuals with human beings.

It's crucial to paste for your thoughts at such times.

Principles:

Life can be a chaotic and overwhelming revel in. The day by day stresses and pressures of labor, relationships, and private responsibilities can take a toll for your highbrow and emotional country. However, that specialize in and following a fixed of requirements will let you live focused and right all the way down to earth inside the midst of existence's chaos.

Principles are the important values that guide your thoughts, actions, and behaviours. They are the critical policies that you follow on your each day lives, guiding you in the direction of your goals and assisting you live actual to yourselves and your beliefs. When you stay your lives in accordance collectively together with your mind, you enjoy greater fulfilled, happier, and extra at peace with yourselves and the area around you.

Having principles is in particular critical for keeping a wholesome thoughts. When you have a smooth set of values and ideals which you observe, you're better capable of address stress, make alternatives that align collectively along with your desires and goals, and revel in extra confident and self-confident to your every day lives.

Furthermore, concepts help you to set obstacles and make choices which might be aligned collectively along with your values and beliefs. This allow you to to keep away from situations which might be risky on your intellectual health and nicely being, which incorporates poisonous relationships, awful conduct, and terrible perception styles.

It's an essential tool for keeping a healthful mind. By dwelling your lives according together along with your values and ideals, you can domesticate extra self-recognition, resilience, and emotional wellness, leading to a happier, extra exciting life.

Defining Principles:

Defining your non-public principles is a important step. It is about records who you're as a person, what drives you, and what you stand for. Principles are basically a set of values that manual your movements and selections in life. They are the muse of your ethical compass.

Chapter 24: What To Do Within The Direction Of Such Instances?

Everyone has someone they respect, or honestly everybody is following the footsteps of a person. Even if you are the primary man or woman who is attempting to acquire any precise goal, there had been many individuals who were first in achieving some desires, and that they've faced pretty a few problems as well.

Make a listing of humans from whom you want to have a look at some aspect. They do now not have to be alive. They may be all people from scientists, politicians, infantrymen, businessmen/businesswomen, a survivor, or a film star.

Read approximately the ones people as a excellent deal as you could, concentrate to their podcasts, watch their interviews, and every distinctive detail which could educate you something about them. Learn from their reports. Notice how they fought adversities.

Whenever you experience caught in a situation, ask your self, what would possibly this person do? How could those human beings cope up with this hassle? What might be their answer?

You can go to this person or a collection of human beings in your thoughts and ask them for recommendation. Name your trouble or emotions, and tell them about it. You can take recommendation from the ones humans and apply it to your existence. These humans can be your non-public advisors. You can ask them for an answer as frequently as you need.

Goals vs Principles

Many parents have goals, whether or not or not it is to shed pounds, maintain extra cash, or beautify in our careers. We create to-do lists, make plans, and set cut-off dates in hopes of reaching those desires. However, on occasion we fall short or lose motivation. This is where requirements come into play. Principles are the essential values and beliefs that guide our movements and choice-making.

Goals can be quick term or long term, and they will be completed thru particular moves taken inside the path of them.

Example:

A purpose is probably to increase income by 10% inside the subsequent area.

This reason is unique, measurable, functionality, relevant, and time-sure.

On the alternative hand, standards are the underlying values and beliefs that manual our desire-making and moves. Principles aren't a few component that may be achieved or completed. Instead, they're the muse upon which we assemble our desires and moves.

Example:

A precept may be to commonly prioritise customer pleasure. This precept courses the selection-making method and movements taken towards reaching the intention of developing income via 10%. Principles make certain that our actions are aligned with our values and beliefs. It lets in human beings be at peace with themselves.

Sometimes the strain of reaching a purpose can also moreover make you lose sight of your ideas. This can reason extra pressure and horrific thoughts.

Living your thoughts is a journey, not a holiday spot, but via taking the time to emerge as aware of and honour your middle principles, you could create a existence that is actual to who you are and what you accept as true with.

Living through your thoughts:

Living your requirements is a critical issue of fundamental a satisfying existence. It's about setting boundaries, residing authentically, and staying actual to your values. However, in a society that regularly encourages us to compromise our ideals and values, it can be tough to stay at the path of internal peace.

Living your ideas way making tough options, taking responsibility to your moves, and status up for what you remember in.

Principles are vital due to the truth they offer a framework for ethical behaviour and choice-making. They will let you expand self-popularity, energy of thoughts, and integrity—all vital features for personal and expert success.

Principles and Inner Peace:

There is a strong connection among your requirements and internal peace. When you stay your ideas, you sense greater aligned with our proper selves, and this brings you a experience of contentment and internal peace. On the alternative hand, at the identical time as we cross in competition on your standards, you experience a sense of pain, unease, and inner turmoil.

Our thoughts are the guiding values and ideals that humans preserve luxurious. They are the muse of your person, and that they help you are making choices and selections which might be in line with your values. When you observe them, you experience a enjoy of authenticity and integrity, it truly is essential for your intellectual and emotional nicely-being.

It moreover enables you prioritise your dreams and aspirations in life. By aligning your actions on the side of your thoughts, you could attention on what truely topics to you and allow pass of distractions and topics that don't serve your higher reason. This readability of cause and reputation can supply a experience of calm and peace in your lives.

In assessment, while you compromise in your ideas, you revel in a enjoy of dissonance and internal warfare. You may enjoy guilt, shame, and regret, that may erode your shallowness and self notion. This can result in strain, anxiety, and different intellectual fitness problems.

Maintaining consistency in living your requirements is a critical step to conducting inner peace. It's no longer enough to absolutely have concepts and values; it is essential to live with the resource of them every day, in every preference, and in each motion you are taking.

Consistency is the critical trouble to building get hold of as proper with and credibility with others. When you usually display your concepts, human beings will come to understand you as someone they may be able to do not forget and depend upon. It moreover permits you live actual to yourself and your beliefs, which may be a powerful deliver of internal peace.

One of the best rewards of living a principled existence is that it lets in you to be real to your self. You don't ought to faux to be a person you aren't, and also you do not should compromise your beliefs or values an excellent manner to fit in or please others.

Another reward is that it permits you to make a top notch impact on the world spherical you. When you stay thru your requirements, you're capable of make picks that replicate your values and ideals, and those selections may additionally have a powerful impact on the human beings and businesses spherical you. Whether it's far volunteering a while, donating to charity, or clearly treating others with kindness and understand, living a principled existence will help you be at peace with yourself.

Principles and ethical dilemmas:

In a worldwide entire of ethical dilemmas, it may every now and then be difficult to keep this way of existence. Ethical dilemmas can rise up in a number of situations and can be specially hard after they include private relationships or professional responsibilities.

When dealing with moral dilemmas, it's far critical to take the time to take into account your options and the capacity outcomes of each one.

You may also furthermore need to are looking for for recommendation from others who share your values or your private advisors, and can undergo in mind extraordinary perspectives.

One manner to method an moral seize 22 scenario is to don't forget the impact your choice might also have on others. Will your selection harm someone else or pass in opposition to their rights? If so, it is vital to bear in mind an opportunity solution that upholds your values at the same time as though respecting the rights of others.

Another method is to recall the prolonged-term outcomes of your choice. Will your preference have horrible outcomes within the destiny? If so, it's essential to don't forget an possibility answer if you want to minimise the potential harm.

Living your thoughts and values is set doing what you don't forget is right, even when it's far difficult. By taking the time to hold in mind your options and are seeking out advice from others, you could make ethical decisions that align together together together with your values and cause internal peace.

Many tremendous people have lived via their necessities and characteristic made a brilliant effect in the international. One of the maximum well-known examples is Mahatma Gandhi. He lived thru the standards of non-violence, reality, and electricity of will. He fought for India's independence from British rule, and his strategies of nonviolent resistance inspired many particular movements throughout the area.

Another example is Nelson Mandela. He come to be imprisoned for 27 years for fighting in the direction of apartheid in South Africa. While in jail, he endured to live thru his requirements of equality, justice, and reconciliation. When he changed into finally released, he have grow to be the primary black president of South Africa and labored tirelessly to promote peace and reconciliation.

Principles and barriers:

Setting limitations and thoughts is essential for defensive your highbrow health. It's crucial to grow to be aware of your non-public barriers and persist with them, in addition to putting in necessities that align with your values and beliefs. These will help you navigate tough conditions and interactions with others, and make certain that you're prioritising your non-public nicely-being.

One way to set limitations is to come to be aware of what behaviours or conditions make you revel in uncomfortable or careworn, and talk those to others. This might in all likelihood imply saying no to effective social engagements that don't align collectively with your values, or putting limits on how tons time you spend enticing with horrible humans or situations.

Chapter 25: Coping

The mind is a effective tool, however it is able to moreover be a deliver of intellectual agony. The constant barrage of thoughts, issues, and anxieties may be overwhelming, leaving us feeling tired and forced. When confronted with intellectual storms, it's important to stay calm and make rational alternatives.

Overanalysing:

Overanalysing is the way of analysing and reanalysing a situation, idea or concept, to the thing of exhaustion. It is a herbal human tendency to excessively study things, however while it turns into a dependancy, it may extensively affect our highbrow fitness.

Overanalysing can bring about stress, anxiety, melancholy, and exclusive intellectual health troubles. It can also affect your preference-making abilties, making it hard so that you can make quick and decisive choices. When you overanalyse, you typically have a tendency to recognition on the horrific factors of a state of affairs and overlook approximately the positives, predominant to a pessimistic outlook on lifestyles.

The outcomes of over analysing may be so excessive that it could show up bodily inside the form of headaches, muscle anxiety, and disrupted sleep. It can also motive a lack of motivation and productiveness, making it tough to carry out even the only of responsibilities.

Some not unusual symptoms of overanalysing embody feeling stuck in a cycle of terrible mind, obsessing over small data and viable outcomes, and feeling together with you can't control your mind or feelings.

You also can additionally find your self continuously trying to find reassurance from others or ruminating on beyond sports.

When you start to understand the ones signs and symptoms, it's miles crucial to reap this to interrupt the cycle of over analysing.

Your mind is continuously bombarded with records, from artwork final dates to non-public commitments, social media notifications to emails. It's no wonder that intellectual muddle and disorganisation can motive emotions of hysteria, stress, and overwhelm you.

Decluttering your thoughts is vital to achieving a enjoy of calm and awareness. Reworking in your highbrow models or techniques of wondering can assist in carrying out calmness.

Mental Models:

Mental models are frameworks that people use to make experience of the sector round them. They are the highbrow constructs people create to help them understand complex situations and make options. However, these fashions can come to be rigid and inflexible over the years, major to overthinking and over analysing.

It can cause a state of mind wherein you turn out to be stuck in a loop of repetitive mind and now not able to shipping ahead. This can take region while your intellectual fashions aren't serving you and also you are not capable of comply them to changing sports.

To prevent this from taking up your highbrow fashions, it is important to frequently compare and replace them. You need to be open to new data and inclined to conform your intellectual fashions to new situations. This may be completed through self-reflection, searching out comments from others, and actively looking for new reviews.

Example:

Optimistic and pessimistic highbrow model or manner of questioning.

When faced with a trouble you do not know the solution to, you may choose out to give up, this is you being a pessimist. Or you may go out of your way and find out a answer and be an optimist.

It's crucial to recognize being an optimist is not healthful. Sometimes it is good enough to give up and flow into on.

Example:

A failed advertising approach that has caused you hundreds of monetary and intellectual troubles. It's ok to prevent operating on it and discover new techniques of beginning a new employer or truely getting a few different procedure.

Anything that reasons you too much highbrow strain want to no longer be given hobby. Stop overthinking about it and attempt to bypass on.

Reframing terrible thoughts is a powerful technique with a view to let you save you overthinking. When you find your self stuck up in terrible questioning, try to step lower decrease back and take a extra reason view of the scenario. Ask yourself questions like: 'Is this without a doubt as awful as I'm making it out to be?' or 'What evidence do I should help this terrible notion?'

Once you have taken a step once more and bought a few mind-set, it is time to reframe your horrible mind. Instead of focusing on the worst-case state of affairs, try to find a extra excellent manner of searching at the state of affairs.

Example:

If you are feeling disturbing about an upcoming presentation, in area of thinking, 'I'm going to debris this up and everyone will anticipate I'm incompetent,' strive wondering, 'I've put in an entire lot of difficult work and practise, and I'm ready to do my splendid.'

Another powerful approach for reframing terrible mind is to guidance gratitude. When you find out yourself caught in a horrible idea pattern, take some moments to popularity on the matters in your existence which you're grateful for. This can help shift your interest from what is going on incorrect to what is going right, and assist you revel in extra effective and constructive common.

Remember, reframing horrible thoughts takes exercise, however it is a powerful device for stopping overthinking and breaking the cycle of bad wondering.

Triage of issues:

1. Walk away for a while.

2. Change what may be modified.

three. Give up or regulate your standards.

No rely what is causing you stress, the answer lies in those three statements. Whenever you are faced with a problem, you may deal with it the usage of this triage.

Example:

You have checks tomorrow, but you aren't simply organized for it. In this example, you can't walk away because of the fact tests are vital. You can't give up because of the truth as a manner to be surrendering with out a fight.

You cannot trade the date of tests this is from your manipulate, but you can manipulate your self. Instead of panicking you can fail, test the maximum critical subjects in a single day as lots as you could and take tests. Whatever takes location subsequent isn't to your manage so do not keep in mind it and put together for the following semester.

Another example is even as your pastime is not permitting you own family time, but it will pay nicely. You can pick out the primary possibility to walk away from your modern-day interest for a miles lots less demanding one although it will pay lots much less. Or you can adjust your mind and consider the exceptional of time you are spending collectively in conjunction with your family in preference to quantity.

Kindness

Kindness is the act of being considerate, useful, and compassionate within the course of others. It includes showing empathy and knowledge closer to others, without looking earlier to a few problem in go lower back. Kindness may be displayed in numerous office work, which consist of a easy smile, a kind word, or a thoughtful deed. Small acts of kindness also can have a terrific impact on others, and they're able to assist to create a amazing and supportive environment.

Kindness isn't only crucial for others, but it is also crucial in your non-public mental peace. When you show kindness to others, it may growth your mood, reduce strain and anxiety, and decorate your common well-being. This is because acts of kindness can reason the discharge of enjoy-well hormones like oxytocin, which promotes emotions of happiness and contentment.

Additionally, at the same time as you are type to others, you're much more likely to get maintain of kindness in move again, that might create a cycle of positivity and goodwill.

In a global which can regularly feel harsh and unforgiving, kindness is greater essential than ever. It can assist to interrupt down obstacles among people, create a revel in of community, and promote information and elegance.

As vital because it's to be type to others, it's far similarly vital to be type to yourself.

Being kind to yourself is one of the maximum crucial matters you can do to your highbrow fitness. People often have a propensity to be their very own maximum harsh critics and keep themselves to unrealistic requirements. This horrible self-talk can bring about anxiety, depression, and different highbrow health problems.

Taking the time to schooling self-compassion and being kind to your self may have a profound impact for your intellectual nicely-being. When you cope with yourself with the affection and kindness that you deserve, you may experience greater confident, high-quality, and at peace with yourself.

Some blessings of being type to yourself encompass advanced self-esteem, reduced pressure tiers, and extended resilience. When you're kind to your self, you are much more likely to attend to your physical and emotional desires, inclusive of getting sufficient sleep, eating nicely, and engaging in sports activities that convey you pride.

One way to schooling self-kindness is to take note of your self-speak. When bad thoughts get up, project them with excessive first-class affirmations.

Example:

If you seize yourself questioning 'I'm no longer appropriate sufficient,' try converting that with 'I am sufficient really as I am.'

Another manner to be type to yourself is to preparation self-care sports that make you experience great. This can be anything from taking a bubble bathtub, reading a ebook, to spending time with friends who make you snort. Whatever it is that brings you joy, ensure you prioritise it for your existence.

Practise Kindness:

1. Compliment a stranger:

Offer a real praise to someone you do no longer realise. It can be as easy as telling them you need their shoes or that they have got a fantastic smile.

2. Volunteer on your network:

Find a close-by organization that aligns collectively along with your interests and volunteer a while. It can be a soup kitchen, animal secure haven, or a charity occasion.

three. Send a handwritten be aware:

Take the time to put in writing a personal word to a person you care approximately. It can be a thanks observe, a word of encouragement, or just a easy 'deliberating you.'

4. Offer to assist:

If you see a person struggling with a few thing, offer to help. It can be carrying groceries, helping with a assignment at art work, or even just paying attention to a person who desires to vent.

Practise Self-Kindness:

Despite education kindness for others, on occasion humans overlook to be kind to themselves.

Example:

When you communicate negatively about your self.

I'm inclined.

I cannot do it.

I will in no way forgive myself.

You have been being unkind to your self.

It's natural to have the ones thoughts, but it's miles now not ok to entertain the ones mind.

Whenever you notice you're being unkind to yourself, save you and tell your self you're being terrible. Talk to yourself with kindness.

Example:

Unkind thought: I'm unpleasant.

Tell your self: I experience like I'm judging myself based mostly on amazing people's perspective. Everyone is adorable and so am I. I love myself certainly the manner I'm.

Breath in slowly and deeply. Notice the air flowing internal and from your lungs. Feel the warmth interior your chest. Imagine your awful thoughts flowing out with each breath and engage with the location round you.

Look on the five devices. Notice their size, form, and texture. Notice the sounds and smells round you. Reach out and sense the devices. Notice the taste to your mouth. If you're inside the agency of someone, be aware of them talking. Notice their voice, their tone, and pitch.

Practise this exercise each time you study you are not being type to yourself.

Positive questioning may have a profound impact to your lives, every bodily and mentally. It has been scientifically established that a extremely good outlook can assist reduce pressure, beautify the immune device, or perhaps result in an prolonged lifespan.

The era at the back of exceptional questioning is rooted within the have a have a examine of neuroscience and psychology. Human mind has the capability to rewire itself, a way called neuroplasticity. This method that you could exchange your belief patterns and ideals, in addition in your bodily behaviours and reactions, thru the usage of deliberately that specialize in exceptional thoughts and reviews.

Research has additionally shown that human feelings and thoughts can effect their bodily fitness. When you're forced and annoying, your our our bodies release cortisol and extraordinary strain hormones that might bring about contamination, weakened immunity, and cause different fitness troubles.

Touch Of Kindness:

Oftentimes you can find out fantastic self-talk isn't always enough to remove unkind mind. In this scenario, soothe yourself with the contact of kindness.

Take slow, deep breaths and exhale. Image the disturbing mind as an item interior your body or to your frame. This object is hurting you, and you ought to perform a little problem to stop it.

First and maximum important, name the unkind feeling.

Example:

Feeling: I'm willing.

Name: I sense like I'm judging via competencies harshly.

Now, take your hand. Imagine it feeling with kindness. It'll soothe your pain. Touch the frame part in that you had imagined the unkind perception is residing. Feel the warm temperature of your skin seeping in through the unkind idea. Focus on your respiratory. Imagine kindness entering your body with each breath and the pain decreasing. Reconnect with the arena round you.

Chapter 26: Rewire Your Memories

Negative recollections may want to have a profound effect for your ordinary nicely-being. They can reason you to feel disturbing, pressured, and depressed. One terrible reminiscence can motive a cascade of negative emotions, major to a vicious cycle that can be tough to break unfastened from.

These feelings also can have an impact on your physical health. Studies have established that people who revel in persistent strain are more likely to be afflicted by quite a few health problems, at the side of weight problems, coronary heart infection, and diabetes. It can also impact your immune system, making it more difficult so as to combat off infections and illnesses.

Desensitisation:

Thoughts have a effective effect on human emotions, behaviours, and ultimately, their lives. When people harbour horrible mind, it is able to reason a lousy outlook on life.

Once you've got a strong emotional reference to a reminiscence, it's far next to not possible to forget approximately approximately it. The suitable information is, you could instruction desensitisation and keep away from poor emotions.

There are three approaches to accumulate it.

Method 1:

The most vital issue is to recognize the horrible feeling. It hurts you emotionally. Name this reminiscence or concept. Think of this reminiscence as an object internal your body. It can be whatever, from a stone to a moon. Notice its size, shape, temperature and so on.

Example:

I'm in no way going to reap lifestyles.

Tell your self: I experience like I'm being judgemental in the path of myself.

Name the horrific feeling object: brick of judgement.

Place it in your frame: internal your chest

Take sluggish deep breaths. The awful feeling is still inner you. Focus for your breaths. Notice the warm temperature of air feeling your lungs. Despite the bad item on your chest, you could even though connect to the arena round you. Look at 5 devices. Notice their duration, shape, shadows. Notice the sounds, scent and tastes. Engage with humans round you. Listen to them cautiously. Notice their expressions, their voice, tone, pitch and so on.

You although have that terrible feeling interior you, however you're able to connect to the world round you.

Method 2:

Sometimes your creativeness can also fail you. In this case you could use a bodily mode to train your mind.

Take out a pen and paper. Write down the terrible concept or memory on the paper and draw the object you had imagined for that feeling. Keep this internet page with you and interact with the vicinity. Look, concentrate, heady scent, flavor and sense. Interact with human beings around you.

By maintaining the picture of negativity with you, you may teach your self to have interaction with the arena even if the unkind feeling is with you. It's about learning a way to address negativity in preference to ignoring it.

Method 3:

Pamper your self:

Pamper day is essentially an afternoon set aside to bask in self-care sports that convey you delight and help you destress.

The sports activities involved in a pamper day can variety from man or woman to person. It can embody sports consisting of taking a bubble bath, getting a rubdown, training yoga, meditating, or genuinely spending time in nature. The secret's to choose out sports that help you loosen up and recharge.

Pamper day is crucial because it permits you to take a wreck from your demanding lives and attention to your properly-being. It helps you to disconnect from the normal noise and distractions spherical you and gives you time to attention on yourselves. By indulging in self-care sports, you may lessen pressure, anxiety, and depression, main to higher intellectual health.

In addition, pamper day furthermore has bodily blessings. Activities consisting of a rub down can help reduce muscle anxiety and beautify blood float, at the same time as yoga and meditation can help beautify flexibility and decrease chronic ache.

Physical touch, together with rubdown or a facial, has been scientifically showed to release endorphins, which are the body's natural revel in-proper chemical substances.

Choose an pastime or a series of sports activities for your self on a specific day of the week. Keep the image of your terrible memories or feelings with you whilst you try and interact in the ones thrilling sports. This will teach your thoughts a way to loosen up even when confronted with annoying mind.

Learn & Live

One common thing that humans generally have a propensity to take delight in in recent times is addictive behaviour. It can be any type of addiction from substance abuse to social media addiction. This can cause immoderate physical and highbrow troubles.

The maximum not unusual cause for addictive behaviour is pressure. When human beings revel in stress, their mind releases a chemical called cortisol, that might trigger emotions of anxiety, despair, and restlessness. This can make them are searching out behaviours or materials that assist them deal with those feelings, which consist of alcohol or drugs or social media.

This behaviour in turn reasons dopamine exhaustion which results in greater awful feeling which in turn triggers humans's addictive behaviour. And the cycle continues.

Stress—> Cortisol release—> Addiction—> Dopamine exhaustion—> Stress

Addictions:

Self-attention is step one in the direction of breaking addictive behaviours.

You want to renowned which you have a hassle and be willing to are attempting to find help. Many individuals who battle with dependancy try and justify their behaviour or blame others for his or her problems. However, this handiest reinforces the addictive behaviour and makes it more hard to triumph over.

If you find out it hard to interrupt free from such behaviours, are attempting to find professional assist. It's vital to undergo in mind that addiction is not a preference, or moral failing, and it's miles in reality not a sign of susceptible thing. Addiction is a complex ailment that impacts the brain and can be brought approximately thru a variety of factors, which consist of genetics, surroundings, and mental fitness problems. Seeking professional help and useful resource is often vital to triumph over addictive behaviours and lead a non violent existence.

Learning:

When it comes to relaxation techniques, many human beings have a tendency to consider sports sports which consist of meditation, yoga, or a hot tub. While the ones are all extraordinary approaches to unwind and de-strain, there's one technique this is frequently overlooked, analyzing new topics.

Learning can provide a very unique enjoy of relaxation and mindfulness that is hard to achieve thru other techniques.

Mindfulness is all approximately being gift within the second and specializing in what is in the the front of you. It permits to lessen pressure and anxiety through the use of allowing you to permit go of problems approximately the beyond or destiny. Learning new matters may be an wonderful manner to schooling mindfulness.

When you look at a few issue new, you want to reputation your interest on the task to be had. You should be truly present inside the second to soak up the data and apprehend it. When you have interaction in learning, your mind releases sense-desirable chemical compounds like dopamine, which allows you sense more comfortable and targeted. This manner of centered attention enables to quiet the thoughts and reduce stress.

When you have a look at, your mind creates new neural pathways that deliver a boost to cognitive feature and reminiscence. These new connections to your mind can help lessen the danger of cognitive decline and get rid of the onset of diseases which include Alzheimer's or dementia.

Furthermore, studying new abilties or taking up a new hobby may additionally have physical blessings which embody superior hand-eye coordination, dexterity, and pleasant motor talents.

Example:

Learning to play a musical device or engaging in sports inclusive of portray or sculpting can help refine your motor skills and improve hand-eye coordination.

Additionally, getting to know new bodily sports activities together with dance, yoga or martial arts can beautify your balance, flexibility, and modern fitness. These sports activities sports also can assist reduce stress and improve your intellectual and emotional properly-being.

Learning Is Self-Care:

Learning may be a shape of self-care that not only advantages your statistics and growth but moreover your rest and mindfulness. When you have got were given interaction in gaining know-how of recent things, you are difficult your mind and breaking from your consolation zones. This can motive a experience of achievement and self belief that absolutely affects your normal well-being.

Additionally, studying can be a calming and meditative hobby. Whether it's miles studying a e-book, taking a web direction, or trying out a modern day interest, the act of mastering calls for attention and attention. This can assist to easy your mind and reduce pressure and anxiety.

Moreover, getting to know can increase your views and boom your information of the sector. This can cause a extra experience of empathy and connection with others, this is vital to your mental and emotional fitness.

Incorporating learning into yourself-care habitual could not have to be time-consuming or pricey. There are many free assets available on line. By taking the time to research some thing new, you are making an investment in yourselves and your properly-being.

What to Learn?

When it involves teaching your self some aspect new, it does now not continually should be academic. You can studies a few issue you experience.

Example:

1. Mindful gardening:

Spending time in nature has been proven to have a relaxing impact at the thoughts and body. Gardening is a extraordinary manner to hook up with nature and take a look at the exceptional flora and flowers that develop to your region.

2. Cooking a latest recipe:

Cooking can be a outstanding way to training mindfulness, as it calls to be able to be completely present and centered on the mission handy. Trying out a new recipe additionally can be a fun manner to take a look at top notch factors and cooking techniques.

three. Learning a modern language:

Learning a modern-day language may be a difficult however profitable experience. It can assist to decorate cognitive characteristic or even postpone the onset of age-related cognitive decline.

four. Reading a e-book:

Reading is a excellent manner to research new topics and get away into some different international. It can be a chilled way to wind down on the stop of the day. This is one of the simplest methods to lessen pressure.

5. Taking an internet direction:

There are many on-line publications available on a terrific sort of topics, from art and pix. Taking a direction can be a splendid manner to look at new talents and extend your understanding, all from the consolation of your home.

Exercise and Mental Health:

Studies have confirmed that one out of four adults and almost eighty one percentage of younger human beings aren't getting enough bodily sports.

Physical hobby has a large form of advantages that pass past really physical fitness. Engaging in normal workout can also assist raise your self notion and self-esteem.

When you workout, your body releases endorphins, that are natural chemical materials that would assist improve your mood and decrease pressure. This assist you to revel in more high fine and confident approximately your self.

Another manner that bodily hobby can enhance your self belief is thru improving your bodily appearance. When you interact in normal exercise, you tone your muscular tissues and improve your body composition. This permits you sense more snug to your own pores and pores and pores and skin and improve yourself-picture.

In addition, putting and conducting fitness dreams also can help enhance your confidence. Whether it's far on foot a 5 km or lifting a positive weight, attaining those desires can offer you with a experience of accomplishment and pleasure on your skills.

If you are trying to decorate your self assurance thru bodily interest, start with the useful resource of setting small and ability desires. This can be some component as smooth as going for a 20-minute stroll every day or joining a newbie's yoga elegance. As you turn out to be extra comfortable, you can progressively increase the intensity and period of your workout workouts.

Chapter 27: Preparing For Cleaning

Before you start cleaning your room, it's important to put together thru manner of amassing all of the important equipment and materials. This will ensure which you have the entirety you need available and can whole the project rapid and efficiently.

Here are some crucial gadgets to have to be had whilst cleaning your room:

1. Trash luggage: for throwing away any items which might be no longer wished or are not in excellent situation.

2. Cleaning materials: which includes all-reason cleaner, glass cleaner, dusting spray, and paper towels.

3. Microfiber cloths: for wiping down surfaces and disposing of dirt.

four. Vacuum purifier: for doing away with dust and debris from carpets and fabric.

5. Broom and dustpan: for sweeping hard floor surfaces.

6. Laundry basket: for accumulating dirty clothes and linens.

7. Organizational packing containers: which incorporates baskets, bins, and drawers, for storing gadgets and preserving your room organized.

Once you've got were given got accrued all of your substances, it is important to make a plan of attack. Decide which regions of your room you want to address first and what duties want to be completed in each area. This will will let you paintings effectively and stay prepared as you smooth.

Additionally, it's far crucial to set aside sufficient time to complete the venture. Cleaning your room can take numerous hours, specifically if it is been some time due to the fact your final deep clean. Make certain to set apart enough time so that you can complete the assignment without feeling rushed or compelled.

By making ready properly, you could ensure that your cleaning efforts are effective and green, and which you are capable of accumulate a clean and properly-maintained room very quickly.

A. Decluttering:

Decluttering is the manner of getting rid of devices which you now not need or use from your dwelling location. This can encompass clothing, books, papers, toys, electronics, and unique possessions which have gathered over time. Decluttering is an crucial step in maintaining a easy and properly-organized room, as it enables to reduce litter and create more area for the belongings you simply use and need.

Here are a few steps that will help you declutter your room successfully:

1. Start by using the use of setting apart a delegated time for decluttering. Choose a time whilst you can artwork undisturbed and if you have sufficient time to finish the task.

2. Create training for your devices: For instance, you may have instructions for clothing, books, papers, toys, and electronics.

3. Sort through your gadgets one category at a time: Decide what you want to preserve, what you need to donate or sell, and what you need to throw away.

4. Use the "12 months rule": If you haven't used an item inside the past year, it is likely that you may now not use it within the future. Consider disposing of gadgets that healthful this criterion.

5. Donate or promote devices in appropriate situation: Instead of throwing away objects which can be although in right state of affairs, remember donating them to a charity or promoting them to recoup some of your cash.

6. Store gadgets you want however do now not use regularly: For gadgets that you want however do not use regularly, recollect storing them in a storage unit, attic, or

basement to unfastened up location to your room.

By following the ones steps, you may effectively declutter your room and create greater area for the stuff you in reality use and want. Decluttering may be a time-eating approach, however it may have a massive effect at the cleanliness and corporation of your residing location. So, take a while, be thorough, and revel in the approach of simplifying your lifestyles.

B. Gathering Cleaning Supplies:

Having the proper cleaning substances available is crucial for effectively cleansing your room. When you have got everything you want at your fingertips, you can clean more effectively and benefit better outcomes. Here are some essential cleansing factors to have to be had whilst cleaning your room:

1. Trash baggage: for throwing away any gadgets which may be not wanted or aren't in accurate circumstance.

2. All-cause purifier: for cleaning a number of surfaces, which incorporates counters, shelves, and fixtures.

three. Glass cleaner: for cleansing domestic windows, mirrors, and other glass surfaces.

4. Dusting spray: for placing off dust and cobwebs from surfaces, which incorporates fixtures, shelves, and baseboards.

five. Microfiber cloths: for wiping down surfaces and getting rid of dirt. Microfiber cloths are superb because of the truth they will be lint-free and do no longer go away streaks.

6. Vacuum cleaner: for eliminating dirt and particles from carpets and upholstery.

7. Broom and dustpan: for sweeping difficult ground surfaces.

8. Laundry basket: for accumulating grimy clothes and linens.

9. Organizational containers: which include baskets, packing containers, and drawers, for

storing objects and retaining your room organized.

It's an first rate concept to have those devices on hand on your room so that you can effects get admission to them each time you want to smooth. If you do not already have the ones devices, you should buy them at your neighborhood hardware or domestic objects keep.

In addition to those objects, remember making an investment in a few specialised cleaning products for unique responsibilities, which incorporates a degreaser for cleaning the kitchen, a tile purifier for the rest room, and a material refresher for eliminating odors from upholstery and bedding. Having those products reachable allow you to deal with unique cleansing responsibilities greater effectively.

By collecting all the crucial cleaning components, you can make certain that you have the whole lot you want to successfully easy your room and maintain a clean and properly-maintained residing vicinity.

C. Setting Cleaning Goals:

Setting cleaning goals will can help you live prepared, recommended, and targeted even as cleansing your room. These dreams will let you prioritize duties and ensure that you address the most crucial responsibilities first. Here are a few steps to help you set cleansing desires:

1. Determine your priorities: Consider what regions of your room need the maximum hobby and what duties may additionally need to have the maximum crucial effect. Focus on the ones areas first.

2. Break down huge responsibilities into smaller, feasible ones: For instance, in region of seeking to clean the complete room in inside the future, ruin the challenge down into smaller, greater viable additives, along with cleansing the surfaces, vacuuming, and organizing.

Chapter 28: Basic Cleaning Techniques

In this phase, we are able to cowl the number one strategies for cleansing your room. These strategies will assist you efficaciously easy severa surfaces and regions of your room, together with home home home windows, mirrors, flooring, and furniture. We also can communicate powerful strategies to take away dirt, dirt, and superb particles, and the manner to preserve a easy and organized residing region. By using those techniques, you may ensure that your room stays easy and nicely-maintained, and that you can revel in a wholesome and snug residing surroundings.

A. Dusting:

Dusting is an vital a part of keeping your room smooth and properly-maintained. Dust can acquire on surfaces, which encompass furnishings, cabinets, and baseboards, and might purpose hypersensitive reactions and respiration problems if now not eliminated often. Here are some pointers for correctly dusting your room:

1. Start from the top: When dusting, it is high-quality to begin from the pinnacle and art work your way down, as dust and debris can choose decrease surfaces as you easy.

2. Use a dusting spray: A dusting spray permit you to successfully cast off dirt from surfaces and save you it from spreading. Simply spray the dusting spray onto a microfiber fabric and wipe down surfaces.

three. Dust in a circular movement: When dusting, use a round movement to make certain that you are correctly casting off dust and particles from all surfaces.

four. Dust regularly: Dust accumulates rapid, so it is critical to dirt your room often, at least as soon as in keeping with week, to preserve it smooth and properly-maintained.

5. Don't neglect tough-to-attain areas: Dust can collect in hard-to-obtain areas, collectively with the tops of shelves and in

tight regions. Be effective to dirt the ones areas frequently to prevent the accumulation of dust and debris.

By using those suggestions and dusting often, you could effectively eliminate dust out of your room and maintain a smooth and properly-maintained dwelling location.

B. Vacuuming:

Vacuuming is an important a part of keeping your room easy and freed from dirt and particles. Vacuuming can correctly dispose of dirt and dust from carpets and rugs, further to pick out out up small debris from difficult floor surfaces. Here are a few suggestions for efficiently vacuuming your room:

1.   Vacuum often: Vacuum your room regularly, at the least as soon as each week, to keep it clean and well-maintained. Regular vacuuming also can growth the existence of your carpet and rugs with the aid of technique of having rid of dust and particles that could reason harm through the years.

2. Start in a nook: When vacuuming, begin in a corner of the room and art work your way out, as this can help you cowl the complete room and choose up all dirt and debris.

three. Vacuum in overlapping strokes: When vacuuming, use overlapping strokes to ensure which you are selecting up all dirt and debris. This may also even assist you keep away from missing any spots.

four. Vacuum excessive-visitors areas first: High-site visitors regions, together with entryways and pathways, will be inclined to get dirtier quicker, so it is important to hoover the ones areas first to make certain that they may be wiped easy efficaciously.

five. Use the proper attachments: Certain vacuuming attachments, which include crevice equipment and fabric brushes, will can help you efficaciously smooth specific regions of your room. Be sure to apply the right attachments for the venture to make certain which you are cleaning efficaciously.

By following those recommendations and vacuuming often, you could successfully take away dust and particles from your room and maintain a easy and properly-maintained living area.

C. Mopping:

Mopping is an critical part of maintaining tough ground surfaces, which incorporates tile and hardwood, easy and nicely-maintained. Mopping can efficiently take away dust, dirt, and super debris, as well as assist maintain the advent and shine of your floor surfaces. Here are a few hints for efficaciously mopping your room:

1. Choose the right mop: There are exquisite sorts of mops to be had, together with string mops, sponge mops, and microfiber mops. Choose a mop this is appropriate in your floor kind and is designed for the form of cleaning you need to do.

2. Use a cleaning solution: A cleansing answer will let you effectively eliminate dust

and debris from your ground surfaces and leave them looking easy and colourful. Choose a cleaning solution this is designed for your floor type and is consistent for the sort of floors you have were given.

three. Start in a corner: When mopping, begin in a nook of the room and paintings your manner out, as this can help you cowl the whole room and select up all dust and particles.

4. Mop in overlapping strokes: When mopping, use overlapping strokes to ensure which you are cleaning the whole ground surface and not lacking any spots.

5. Let the cleaning answer sit: After utilizing the cleansing solution, allow it sit down for a couple of minutes to permit it to correctly cast off dirt and debris. This may additionally assist save you streaks and depart your ground looking easy and vibrant.

6. Change the water regularly: Dirty water can spread dirt and debris, so it is crucial to

change the water frequently on the identical time as mopping. This will help make sure that you are cleansing efficaciously and no longer spreading dirt and debris spherical your room.

By following these recommendations and mopping often, you could efficaciously eliminate dust and particles out of your ground surfaces and keep a easy and well-maintained living vicinity.

D. Wiping Down Surfaces:

Wiping down surfaces, collectively with countertops, tables, and desks, is an crucial a part of preserving your room clean and properly-maintained. Wiping down surfaces can effectively get rid of dirt, dust, and unique particles, in addition to help maintain the advent and cleanliness of these surfaces. Here are a few suggestions for correctly wiping down surfaces to your room:

1. Choose the proper cleansing solution: A cleaning answer assist you to efficaciously

dispose of dirt and particles from surfaces and leave them searching smooth and shiny. Choose a cleaning solution this is designed for the form of ground you are cleansing and is secure for that ground.

2. Gather critical materials: In addition to a cleaning solution, you will additionally need cleaning cloths or paper towels, and a bucket or spray bottle to hold the cleansing answer. Choose components that are suitable for the form of floor you are cleansing.

3. Start on the pinnacle: When wiping down surfaces, start at the top and artwork your way down, as this could help you avoid spreading dust and debris during the room.

4. Wipe in a round movement: When wiping down surfaces, use a round movement to make sure that you are successfully eliminating dirt and particles. This may even help save you streaks and depart the surface searching clean and colourful.

five. Pay interest to corners and crevices: Be positive to smooth corners and crevices, as dirt and particles can accumulate in the ones areas. Use a cleaning device, which include a toothbrush or Q-tip, to smooth the ones regions efficaciously.

6. Wipe down frequently-touched surfaces regularly: Frequently-touched surfaces, which include doorknobs and mild switches, will be inclined to get grimy faster, so it's miles vital to wipe them down often to ensure that they'll be clean and free of dust and particles.

By following those pointers and wiping down surfaces often, you can correctly dispose of dust and particles from the ones surfaces and keep a smooth and nicely-maintained residing region.

E. Laundry:

Doing laundry is an crucial a part of maintaining your room easy and prepared. Here are a few suggestions for efficiently doing laundry:

1. Sort clothes with the useful resource of color: Before washing clothes, type them into piles primarily based mostly on shade, as this could assist prevent color bleeding and make sure that garments are frivolously wiped clean.

2. Choose the right detergent: Choose a detergent this is appropriate for the type of garments you're washing and is regular for the fabric.

three. Follow care labels: Care labels on clothing provide essential facts about a manner to nicely take care of the garments. Follow the ones labels at the same time as washing clothes to make sure that they'll be wiped easy successfully and do no longer get damaged.

Chapter 29: Deep Cleaning Tasks

In addition to normal cleaning, it is also vital to perform deep cleaning responsibilities periodically so you can hold a easy and nicely-maintained room. Deep cleansing responsibilities are greater thorough and immoderate than everyday cleaning obligations and are designed to clean regions that may be not noted inside the course of everyday cleaning. Examples of deep cleaning responsibilities encompass cleansing the inner of shelves and drawers, cleansing the bathroom and kitchen, and deep-cleansing carpets and material. In this section, we are capable of discover those deep cleansing responsibilities in extra element.

A. Cleaning the Bathroom:

Cleaning the rest room is a important part of maintaining your room and domestic clean. The relaxation room is a excessive-web website online web page traffic vicinity that could rapid emerge as cluttered and grimy, so it's miles important to easy it frequently and punctiliously. Here are a few hints for cleansing the toilet:

1. Start thru way of decluttering: Remove any objects that don't belong within the rest room and area them in their proper garage locations.

2. Gather cleaning materials: You will need cleansing elements which includes a bucket, cleansing cloths, scrub brush, and cleaning products along with an all-purpose cleanser, rest room bowl cleanser, and glass cleaner.

3. Clean the rest room: Begin via cleansing the toilet bowl and then waft at once to the outdoor of the relaxation room, which consist of the base, tank, lid, and deal with.

4. Clean the sink, counter tops, and mirrors: Use a cleaning product to smooth the sink, countertops, and mirrors, ensuring to get rid of any cleaning cleaning soap scum or water spots.

five. Clean the shower and tub: Use a scrub brush and cleansing product to easy the shower and tub, ensuring to put off any cleansing cleaning soap scum, mold, and dust.

6. Mop the ground: Mop the bathroom ground to eliminate any dust and dust.

By following the ones steps and regularly cleaning the rest room, you could make sure that it stays easy and hygienic.

B. Cleaning the Kitchen:

The kitchen is each one-of-a-kind immoderate-site visitors region that requires everyday cleansing with the intention to maintain a clean and hygienic area. Here are some tips for cleaning the kitchen:

1. Start through the usage of decluttering: Remove any items that don't belong inside the kitchen and location them of their proper garage locations.

2. Gather cleaning materials: You will need cleaning materials along side a bucket, cleansing cloths, scrub brush, and cleaning merchandise which incorporates an all-reason

cleanser, grease-reducing cleanser, and glass cleanser.

3. Clean the sink: Use a cleaning product to easy the sink, making sure to eliminate any food residue and water spots.

four. Clean the counter tops: Use a cleansing product to easy the countertops, ensuring to do away with any food residue and grease.

5. Clean the range: Use a cleansing product and scrub brush to smooth the stove, ensuring to remove any grease and meals residue.

6. Clean the oven: Use a cleaning product and scrub brush to smooth the inner of the oven, ensuring to put off any meals residue and grease.

7. Mop the floor: Mop the kitchen floor to put off any dust and dust.

By following the ones steps and often cleaning the kitchen, you may make sure that it stays clean and hygienic.

C. Cleaning Windows and Mirrors:

Cleaning windows and mirrors is an important part of maintaining a easy and prepared room. Here are some pointers for cleansing home windows and mirrors:

1. Gather cleaning components: You will want cleansing materials together with a bucket, cleaning cloths, squeegee, and cleansing merchandise together with a window purifier and glass purifier.

2. Clean the residence home windows: Use a window cleaner and cleansing fabric to easy the windows, ensuring to put off any dirt, dirt, and fingerprints.

three. Clean the mirrors: Use a glass cleanser and cleaning material to easy the mirrors, making sure to do away with any streaks and fingerprints.

four. Use a squeegee: After cleansing the home domestic windows and mirrors, use a squeegee to remove any more water and to save you streaks.

By following those steps and frequently cleansing home windows and mirrors, you could make sure that they continue to be smooth and streak-loose.

D. Cleaning Furniture and Upholstery:

Cleaning fixtures and fabric is critical if you want to maintain a smooth and snug room. Here are some hints for cleansing furniture and material:

1. Check the care label: Before cleansing fixtures and cloth, check the care label for any specific commands or recommendations.

2. Vacuum: Use a vacuum purifier to take away any dirt and particles from fixtures and cloth.

three. Spot clean: Use a cleansing product and a easy cloth to identify clean any stains or spills on furnishings and fabric.

4. Use the right cleansing method: Depending on the sort of furniture and fabric, you could want to use a one-of-a-type

cleaning method, along side steam cleaning or dry cleansing.

5. Protect: After cleansing fixtures and material, bear in mind using a protector to assist save you destiny stains and spills.

By following the ones steps and often cleansing fixtures and material, you can make sure that they stay smooth and in proper scenario.

Organizing Your Room:

Organizing your room assist you to preserve it easy and tidy, and make it less complicated to find what you need at the same time as you need it. This segment will cover a few suggestions and strategies for organizing your room, at the side of decluttering, the usage of garage solutions, and growing a tool for maintaining your room tidy. Whether you are trying to simplify your existence, beautify your residing location, or definitely get more prepared, this segment will offer you with the machine you want to get commenced out.

A. Making the Most of Your Space:

When it consists of organizing your room, making the most of your vicinity is high. Here are some recommendations for maximizing your garage options and developing a practical, organized dwelling vicinity:

1. Measure your room and furnishings: Before you start organizing, diploma your room and the devices you want to keep in it. This will help you decide the splendid placement for fixtures and garage solutions, and make sure that the entirety suits.

2. Utilize vertical place: Make use of vertical region through the use of putting in cabinets, putting hooks, or including a bookshelf. This allows you to keep more gadgets in your room with out taking up treasured ground region.

three. Consider multipurpose furnishings: Furniture that serves a couple of purpose, together with a garage ottoman or a bed with incorporated drawers, can help you make the most of your location. These gadgets not only serve a beneficial cause, however additionally loose up ground space that would otherwise be taken up with the beneficial resource of separate pieces of furniture.

four. Purge often: Regularly go through your gadgets and purge a few element which you no longer want or use. This will help you hold your area litter-loose, and make it less complicated to discover what you need at the same time as you want it.

five. Get creative with garage answers: Don't be afraid to get modern at the side of your storage solutions. Use hooks to save luggage and hats, installation a pegboard for device and utensils, or upload baskets or packing containers for smaller gadgets.

By making the most of your region and utilizing storage answers that be clearly right for you, you may create a functional, prepared dwelling area that is simple to keep.

B. Creating a Closet System:

A properly-organized closet system need to make a huge difference within the simple appearance and functionality of your room. Here are some suggestions for growing a closet device that works for you:

1. Assess your closet: Take a have a have a examine your closet and verify what gadgets you need to keep and what forms of garage answers will work superb on your desires.

2. Maximize place: Utilize the general top of your closet with the useful aid of adding shelves, placing rods, and hooks. This will assist you maximize your storage alternatives and maintain your objects organized.

three. Utilize drawer and shelf dividers: Keep smaller gadgets prepared by way of manner of using drawer and shelf dividers. This will assist you maintain your gadgets separated and prevent them from becoming tangled or misplaced.

4. Group similar gadgets together: Group similar gadgets together, which includes all of

your shirts in a unmarried segment, pants in any other, and so forth. This will make it a good deal much less hard to discover what you want and preserve your gadgets prepared.

five. Purge regularly: Regularly undergo your closet and purge some thing which you now not want or use. This will keep your closet free of muddle and make it much less tough to look what objects you have got and what you can need to buy inside the future.

By following those guidelines, you can create a closet gadget this is every beneficial and fashionable. Not high-quality will it help you maintain your items organized, but it's going to additionally offer you with a experience of pleasure and peace of thoughts whenever you open your closet.

In order to maximize the space in your closet, endure in thoughts including shelving gadgets and hooks. This will offer you with extra storage options and assist you maintain devices off the ground, which also can make your closet look large.

When it includes organizing your closet, there are some of extraordinary alternatives available, together with:

1. Hanging rod organizers: These organizers let you maximize the gap to your closet with the beneficial aid of providing more setting rods for clothes, luggage, and one-of-a-kind devices.

2. Shelf dividers: Shelf dividers are a exquisite manner to maintain your devices prepared and prevent them from turning into tangled or falling over. They are especially useful for gadgets like shoes, luggage, and folded garments.

three. Drawer organizers: Drawer organizers are wonderful for keeping smaller items like socks, underclothes, and jewelry prepared and smooth to discover.

four. Hanging shoe organizers: Hanging shoe organizers may be hung on the lower back of the closet door and are an fantastic manner to shop shoes and other small gadgets, at the same time as releasing up ground location.

When organizing your closet, it is also crucial to business enterprise comparable gadgets collectively. For instance, you could preserve all your shirts in a single segment, pants in a few other, and so forth. This will make it simpler to find out what you want and keep your devices prepared.

Finally, it is essential to frequently undergo your closet and purge something that you no longer want or use. This will assist you maintain your closet free of clutter and make it lots much less complicated to look what objects you've got got and what you can want to purchase within the future.

By taking the ones steps, you can create a closet gadget that is each realistic and stylish, and will help you preserve your gadgets organized and clean to find out.

C. Organizing Your Desk

Organizing your table is a important step in maintaining your room clean and muddle-free. A well-prepared table can beautify your productiveness and decrease strain. Here are a few recommendations for organizing your desk:

1. Declutter: Start with the useful resource of disposing of everything out of your desk and sorting via it. Keep simplest what you need and discard or recycle the rest.

2. Assign a location for the whole lot: Decide in which each item will skip to your desk. Designate particular spots for pens, paper, and unique materials to avoid clutter and maintain subjects tidy.

3. Use desk organizers: Desk organizers like trays, record holders, and pencil cups can help preserve your desk neat and tidy.

4. Keep regularly used gadgets indoors reap: Keep devices you operate regularly, like a cellphone, stapler, and pocket e-book,

interior arm's obtain for easy get admission to.

5. Store less frequently used items out of sight: Items you don't use as frequently, like greater paper or folders, may be saved in a close-by cabinet or on a shelf to keep your table muddle-loose.

6. Label everything: Label drawers, trays, and specific storage areas to help you short and effects find out what you want.

7. Establish a submitting system: Set up a filing device to preserve crucial papers and documents prepared. This can be as easy as a document folder or a more elaborate cupboard tool.

By following the ones steps, you may create a properly-organized desk in case you want to make it much less difficult to reputation to your paintings and decrease stress.

D. Storing Items in a Neat and Tidy Way

Storing devices in a neat and tidy way is an critical element of retaining your room smooth. Here are some hints to help you keep devices in a way that is every efficient and aesthetically beautiful:

1. Assess your storage goals: Determine how masses storage you want and what form of storage would fantastic healthful your desires. For instance, do you want a dresser, closet organizers, or shelving devices?

2. Make use of vertical area: Utilize the vertical area in your room by using adding shelving devices or placing organizers. This will help you are making the maximum of your available vicinity and reduce muddle on your floor.

3. Label the entirety: Label boxes, boxes, and precise storage packing containers to make it easy to find what you need.

Chapter 30: Maintaining A Clean Room

Maintaining a clean room is critical to making sure that the benefits of getting a easy room are sustained over time. In this segment, we are capable to talk guidelines and techniques to help you preserve a easy room and maintain it looking its tremendous. This consists of developing a cleaning regular, staying organized, and addressing spills and messes as speedy as they upward push up. By following those guidelines, you could preserve your room easy, prepared, and clutter-loose.

A. Establishing a Cleaning Schedule

Establishing a cleaning schedule is an crucial step in retaining a easy room. A well-designed cleansing time desk will can help you stay on top of messes, restriction muddle, and ensure that your living place is continuously so as. To create an powerful cleaning time table, begin via manner of list all the responsibilities that need to be accomplished to preserve your room clean, together with dusting, vacuuming, wiping down surfaces, doing laundry, and deep cleansing duties like cleansing the relaxation room and kitchen. Then, determine how frequently each venture desires to be finished and allocate the critical time because of this. For example, you can want to dirt your room as soon as in line with week and vacuum instances every week.

Consider your manner of existence and agenda even as growing your cleansing time desk. If you're a busy person, you can want to allocate shorter periods of time for cleaning duties each day so that you can get the whole lot finished with out feeling overwhelmed. If you have got were given more loose time, you may need to do a greater thorough cleansing on a weekly foundation.

It's critical to be realistic approximately how loads time you could allocate to cleaning each week and to regulate your agenda as wanted. If you discover that your cleaning time table is virtually too traumatic, remember simplifying it or locating techniques to make the duties greater green. You also can consider breaking down big cleaning responsibilities into smaller, greater capability chunks.

Finally, keep on in conjunction with your cleaning time table and make it a dependancy. This assist you to preserve a easy and organized room for the prolonged-term and make certain that you are continually surrounded by a clutter-free and interesting surroundings.

An example of a cleaning time table is as follows:

Monday: Dust surfaces, vacuum ground, wipe down lavatory surfaces

Tuesday: Laundry day, clean home windows and mirrors

Wednesday: Mop ground, smooth kitchen counters and domestic system

Thursday: Organize closet, tidy up desk

Friday: Deep clean the rest room

Saturday: Tackle a deep cleaning assignment (which incorporates furniture and cloth)

Sunday: Relax day, take a look at development and regulate time desk as wanted.

B. Quick Cleaning Tips for Busy Days

1. Keep a designated cleaning caddy with vital materials with out problems available.

2. Tackle one venture at a time and prioritize based totally on urgency and time availability.

three. Utilize multi-reason cleaners for green cleansing.

four. Keep surfaces decluttered to reduce cleaning time.

five. Use disposable wipes for short cleanups.

6. Don't neglect about regularly-forgotten areas like moderate fixtures, baseboards, and door handles.

7. Divide and triumph over via delegating cleaning obligations to family people.

8. Create a "10-minute tidy" everyday in advance than bed to cease each day on a clean have a look at.

C. Encouraging Others to Help with Cleaning

When it involves cleaning a room, it is critical to involve others, specially in case you stay with others. Sharing the duties now not best makes the cleaning technique much less complicated however moreover helps to foster a feel of network and responsibility among folks who live in the area. In this phase, we're able to explore specific techniques to encourage others to assist with cleaning.

1. Lead with the aid of manner of example: Demonstrate a easy and organized room to others and maintain it regularly. This units a extremely good instance and encourages others to do the identical.

2. Assign age-suitable duties to children: Children can be taught the importance of retaining their room easy and tidy. Assign duties which is probably appropriate to their age and abilities, which includes making their mattress or setting away toys.

3. Set clean expectancies: Clearly communicate what's expected of every member of the family in terms of preserving the house easy. This includes assigning unique cleansing duties and putting a timeline for of entirety.

4. Create a reward device: Motivate family contributors through the usage of growing a reward gadget for a interest nicely finished. This may be as simple as giving praise or profitable them with a special deal with.

five. Foster a revel in of shared ownership: Encourage a sense of shared ownership and teamwork in retaining a easy home. Remind family individuals that everybody's efforts contribute to the overall cleanliness of the house.

6. Regularly communicate about cleansing desires: Hold regular meetings to discuss cleaning goals and development. This permits keep anyone on the identical web page and encourages collaboration.

7. Provide crucial assets: Ensure that everyone has access to the necessary property, which include cleaning substances and tools, to make cleaning much less complicated. This allows make cleansing a much less daunting mission and encourages participation.

eight. Show appreciation: Show appreciation and renowned individual efforts in the direction of retaining the house clean. This allows to enhance morale and encourages persevered participation.

D. Dealing with Common Cleaning Challenges

Cleaning a room can be a frightening task, and it's far everyday to encounter challenges along the manner. Whether it's miles managing litter, keeping a easy area, or finding the inducement to begin cleansing, it's miles vital to have techniques in area to overcome those disturbing situations. In this phase, we can have a observe a few commonplace cleaning traumatic situations and provide recommendations and tricks that will help you conquer them.

1. Clutter: One of the maximum common cleansing demanding situations is dealing with muddle. To overcome this assignment, start with the resource of the use of decluttering your room often, donate items you not need, and recall storage answers to maintain your devices prepared.

2. Lack of motivation: Another commonplace task is a lack of motivation. To conquer this task, set practical cleaning goals, make cleansing a dependancy, and find techniques to make cleaning thrilling, collectively with being attentive to music or walking with a chum.

three. Time constraints: For humans with busy schedules, locating time to clean may be a assignment. To overcome this mission, installation a cleaning time table and prioritize cleaning duties, focusing at the most crucial responsibilities first.

4. Cleaning merchandise: Some humans war with the overwhelming kind of cleansing products available. To conquer this assignment, stick to a few fundamental merchandise, including all-cause cleaner, and keep away from searching for products that are not essential.

five. Dealing with messes: Messes are a common project in any room. To triumph over this venture, cope with messes as soon as they arise and characteristic a plan in area for cleaning up spills or accidents rapid.

By addressing those not unusual cleaning annoying situations, you may be able to keep your room easy and tidy pretty sincerely. Remember, consistency is fundamental, so make cleansing a addiction and hold on collectively with your cleansing time table.

www.ingramcontent.com/pod-product-compliance
Lightning Source LLC
Chambersburg PA
CBHW071440080526
44587CB00014B/1934